PELICAN BOOKS

COMMUNICATIONS

Raymond Williams was born in 1921 in the Welsh border village of Pandy. His father was a railway signalman. He was educated at the village school, at Abergavenny Grammar School, and at Trinity College, Cambridge. After the war, in which he served as an anti-tank captain in the Guards Armoured Division, he became an adult education tutor in the Oxford University Delegacy for Extra-Mural Studies until 1961, when he was elected Fellow of Jesus College, Cambridge, where he was elected Professor of Drama in 1974. In 1947 he edited *Politics and Letters*. His books include *Drama in Performance* (1954), *Culture and Society 1780–1950* (1958), *Border Country*, a novel (1960), *The Long Revolution* (1961), *Second Generation* (1964), *Modern Tragedy* (1966), *Drama from Ibsen to Brecht* (1968), *The Country and the City* (1973), *Television Technology and Cultural Form* (1974) and *Keywords* (1976).

Raymond Williams is married and has three children.

GW00642595

RAYMOND WILLIAMS

COMMUNICATIONS

*

THIRD EDITION

PENGUIN BOOKS

Penguin Books Ltd, Harmondsworth, Middlesex, England
Penguin Books, 625 Madison Avenue, New York, New York 10022, U.S.A.
Penguin Books Australia Ltd, Ringwood, Victoria, Australia
Penguin Books Canada Ltd, 2801 John Street, Markham, Ontario, Canada L3R 1B4
Penguin Books (N.Z.) Ltd, 182–190 Wairau Road, Auckland 10, New Zealand

—

First published in Penguin Books 1962
Revised edition published by Chatto & Windus 1966
Published in Pelican Books 1968
Reprinted 1970, 1971, 1973
Third edition 1976
Reprinted 1977, 1980, 1982

—

—

Set, printed and bound in Great Britain by
Cox & Wyman Ltd, Reading
Set in Monotype Baskerville

CONTENTS

Foreword   7

1. Definitions   9
2. History   14
3. Content   28
4. Controversy   104
5. Proposals   138

Retrospect and Prospect, 1975   180
Further Reading   190

FOREWORD

THIS book was first published in 1962 as a Penguin Special. A new edition, revised and updated, was published in 1966. The present edition is again fully revised and updated, and includes a new section, 'Retrospect and Prospect, 1975', which reviews the general development of the subject since the book was first written and tries to identify some of the major issues with which we are likely to be faced in the years ahead. At the same time, while including these revisions and additions, I have tried as far as possible to sustain the scope and intention of the book, as it was first conceived in 1960. The intervening years, while bringing a number of changes, seem only to have confirmed the continuing need for this kind of analysis and argument.

My wife's help has been central in all three editions. I wish still to acknowledge the initiative of the National Union of Teachers in calling the 1960 conference on 'Popular Culture and Personal Responsibility' which was in a practical way the book's starting point. I have also been helped, at different times and in different ways, by Dieter Pevsner, Stuart Hall, Graham Martin, Richard Hoggart, Elias Bredsdorff, Martin Bernal, Ederyn Williams and Nicholas Garnham. I am especially grateful to Madawc Williams for his work on the 1973 content analysis of the press. Some of the new material in Chapter 3 first appeared in *The Listener*.

R.W.

CHAPTER ONE

DEFINITIONS

WHAT do we mean by communication? The oldest meaning of the word, in English, can be summarized as the passing of ideas, information, and attitudes from person to person. But, later, communication came also to mean a line or channel from place to place. Since the Industrial Revolution there has been so much improvement in this kind of communication – in canals, railways, steamships, cars, aircraft – that often, when we say communications, we mean these ways of travelling and carrying. Yet there is another major line of modern improvement and invention. Steam printing, the electric telegraph, photography, wireless, film, television are new ways of passing ideas, information, and attitudes from person to person, and we call these, also, communications. So that now the word has different meanings in common use, and there is often confusion between them. I think that for describing the physical means of travelling and carrying, our other word, transport, is better than communications, but I suppose both will go on being used. In any case, in this book, I mean by communications the institutions and forms in which ideas, information, and attitudes are transmitted and received. I mean by communication the process of transmission and reception.

In our own generation, there has been a dramatic tightening of interest in this world of communications. The development of powerful new means of communication has coincided, historically, with the extension of democracy and with the attempts, by many kinds of ruling group, to control and manage democracy. The development has also coincided with important changes in the nature of work and in education, which have given many people new kinds of social opportunity. There has been a great expansion in the scale of ordinary society, both through the new communications systems and through the growth of many kinds of large-scale organization. Acting together, these developments have created social problems which seem to be of a quite new kind.

The growth of interest in communications is an important response to this new situation. It came, really, as a breakthrough in experience, cutting across our usual categories. Already some of our basic ideas of society are being changed by this new emphasis. From one familiar approach, through traditional politics, we have seen the central facts of society as power and government. From another familiar approach, through traditional economics, we have seen the central concerns of society as property, production, and trade. These approaches remain important, but they are now joined by a new emphasis: that society is a form of communication, through which experience is described, shared, modified, and preserved. We are used to descriptions of our whole common life in political and economic terms. The emphasis on communications asserts, as a matter of experience, that men and societies are not confined to relationships of power, property, and production. Their relationships in describing, learning, persuading, and exchanging experiences are seen as equally fundamental. This emphasis is exceptionally important in the long crisis of twentieth-century society. Many people, starting from older versions of society, have seen the growth of modern communications not as an expansion of men's powers to learn and to exchange ideas and experiences, but as a new method of government or a new opportunity for trade. All the new means of communication have been abused, for political control (as in propaganda) or for commercial profit (as in advertising). We can protest against such uses, but unless we have a clear alternative version of human society, we are not likely to make our protests effective.

My own view is that we have been wrong in taking communication as secondary. Many people seem to assume as a matter of course that there is, first, reality, and then, second, communication about it. We degrade art and learning by supposing that they are always second-hand activities: that there is life, and then afterwards there are these accounts of it. Our commonest political error is the assumption that power – the capacity to govern other men – is the reality of the whole social process, and so the only context of politics. Our commonest economic error is the assumption that production and trade are our only practical activities, and that they require no other human justification or scrutiny. We need to say what many of us know in experience: that the life of man, and the business of society, cannot be confined to these ends; that the struggle to learn, to describe, to understand, to educate, is a central and necessary part of our humanity. This struggle is not begun, at second hand, after reality has occurred. It is, in itself, a major way in which reality is continually formed and changed. What we call society is not only a network of political and economic arrangements, but also a process of learning and communication.

Communication begins in the struggle to learn and to describe. To start this process in our minds, and to pass on its results to others, we depend on certain communication models, certain rules or conventions through which we can make contact. We can change these models, when they become inadequate, or we can modify and extend them. Our efforts to do so, and to use the existing models successfully, take up a large part of our living energy. The history of a language is a record of efforts of this kind, and is as central a part of the history of a people as its changing political and

economic institutions. Moreover, many of our communication models become, in themselves, social institutions.
Certain attitudes to others, certain forms of address, certain
tones and styles, become embodied in institutions which are
then very powerful in social effect. The crisis in modern communications has been caused by the speed of invention and
by the difficulty of finding the right institutions in which
these technical means are to be used. In modern Britain, we
have a whole range of uses of printing, of photography, of
television, which do not necessarily follow from the technical
means themselves. Many have been shaped by changing
political and economic forces. Many, also, have been shaped
by what are really particular communication models: the
idea that speaking or writing to many people at once is
speaking or writing to 'the masses'; the idea that there are
clear types of people and interest – 'Light Programme',
'Third Programme', and 'Home Service' (now Radios 1, 3
and 4); 'popular' and 'quality' – that we can separate and
label. These arguable assumptions are often embodied in
solid practical institutions, which then teach the models from
which they start. We cannot examine the process of general
communication in modern society without examining the
shapes of these institutions. Further, if we understand the importance of communication, in all our social activities, we
find that in examining the process and the institutions we are
also looking at our society – at some of our characteristic
relationships – in new ways.

This book is an introduction to this field of inquiry. It
begins with an outline of the history of our modern means and
institutions of communication. It goes on to examine, in
various ways, some of the methods and content of some of our
most important institutions. It then passes to the very lively
arguments and controversies which have sprung up around
these institutions, and which seem to be extending and in-

tensifying year by year, as the sense of crisis mounts. It turns finally to a series of suggestions and proposals, which can be used as a basis for a general discussion of possible developments and changes.

I have been working in this field now for many years, and I am very conscious of the difficulties involved in any short book on so complicated and controversial a subject. So far as possible, I have based the book on methods of teaching which I used over several years in classes for members of the Workers' Education Association and for trade unionists. The object, in such teaching, was not only to present certain facts and methods of study, but also to start a process of independent inquiry and common discussion. I hope that the book can be used in these same ways, for a kind of communication which I believe to be valuable.

I said in *Culture and Society*: 'I shall be glad to be answered, in whatever terms . . . When we consider how matters now stand, our continuing interest and language could hardly be too lively.' I have greatly valued the very many answers I actually received, agreeing and disagreeing. The original invitation stands.

CHAPTER TWO

HISTORY

THE printed book is the first great means of modern communication. Writing had made possible the recording of communication; printing made possible its rapid distribution. In England there were two or three printers in 1500, but by 1600 more than ninety. Thirteen titles were printed in 1510, but by 1600 an annual average of about 150. The printing of ballads, almanacs, and pamphlets also increased at a rapid rate. In the seventeenth century the ordinary edition of a book was about 2,000 copies, while a popular almanac sold an average of 16,000 copies.

Between 1500 and 1700 many attempts to regulate printing were made by the State. A form of censorship was set up in 1538; the number of printing houses was several times limited by patent; offending authors were liable to prosecution. These measures fluctuated with a changing political history. As printing moved towards the newspaper, severe measures were taken. In 1662 a Licensing Act limited the number of printers, to prevent 'abuses', and in 1663 a Surveyor of the Press was appointed, with a virtual monopoly in printed news. Parliament's refusal to renew this Licensing Act in 1695 led to a rapid expansion of newspapers and magazines. The history of communications from 1700 until our own century is largely the history of the Press. From the slowly improving postal services to the coming of railways and telegrams, this expansion was dependent on general communications. The use of steam printing, from 1814, decisively raised the rate of distribution, and the effect of subsequent changes in printing, including major changes now taking place, is profound.

By the early nineteenth century, the annual sale of newspapers was about twenty-four million, and some 580 books were published each year, in ordinary editions of about 1,000. Between 1700 and 1820, however, there had been repeated attempts, in new forms, to control what was printed. There was extensive Government bribery of journalists, and certain compliant newspapers were subsidized. Direct State control was replaced by forms of market tax: the Stamp Duty, on every newspaper page, and the Advertisement Tax. These were not to raise revenue but to 'suppress libels'. Starting at a halfpenny in the early eighteenth century, Stamp Duty had risen to fourpence by 1815, the steep rise mainly in the later years, in direct relation to the growth of radical opinion. Independent journalists fought back, even after the further imposition, in 1819, of formal Acts directly aimed at suppressing freedom of expression.

After the Reform Bill of 1832, the situation changed. The tax on advertisements was reduced in 1833 and abolished in 1853. Stamp Duty was reduced in 1836 and abolished in 1855. These developments, aided by the growth of steam printing and railways, led to a further and more rapid expansion. Sales of newspapers rose by 33 per cent between 1816 and 1836, by 70 per cent between 1836 and 1856, and by some 600 per cent between 1856 and 1882. From the 1830s, the new Sunday newspapers, dealing mainly in reports of crime and sensational fiction, took a lead over daily newspapers which they have never lost. By 1850 the daily papers were being read by one adult in eighty, the Sunday papers by one adult in twenty. By 1900 the daily papers were read by one adult in five or six, the Sunday papers by one adult in three. There was a comparable expansion in the reading of magazines, and a slower expansion in the reading of books. The annual production of some 580 books in 1810 had become 2,600 in the 1850s and reached 6,000 by 1901. Editions had become larger and prices were lower.

We must now turn to another line of development, in the theatre and in forms of entertainment. The first theatres were built in England in the 1570s, but there had been a popular drama before this, in the guild plays – miracles and moralities – performed at festivals in the streets and market-places. Beside these, there was a body of popular entertainment, given by travelling professional performers, at fairs and similar occasions, often with difficulty from the law, which normally treated them as rogues and vagabonds. The importance of the new theatres of the 1570s was that some of these professionals at last found a home, though the theatres remained under constant pressure from the authorities, and the companies had to seek patronage and protection to survive. Over forty years (then declining before the Puritan closures of the 1640s) there was a remarkable cultural growth, in which the professional actors and the new professional dramatists found a popular audience. Other forms of professional entertainment continued under the usual difficulties.

When the theatres were reopened in 1660, there was a new kind of division. There were to be only two Royal Patent Theatres, and these were to have a monopoly of what thus came to be called 'legitimate' drama. Other kinds of professional entertainer had survived, and in the eighteenth century, while many continued to tour the fairs, others found their way into new kinds of theatre – the 'illegitimate' world of pantomime, spectacle, and variety. The monopoly of the Patent Theatres was not broken until as late as 1843. It had done much to enforce the idea of two separate traditions of performance, one 'art' and one 'entertainment'. Yet the dividing line had never been clear, and there had been some expansion of theatres.

In 1600, at the height of the Elizabethan drama, there were at least six theatres in London. In 1700, after the narrowing of the Restoration, there were only two. By 1750, five London theatres and five in the provinces had grown up alongside the Patent Theatres, and by 1800 the number in the provinces had reached forty. By 1850 there were twenty-one theatres in London, and seventy-five in the provinces. The real expansion came between 1850 and 1900, and at the end of it there were sixty-three theatres in London and more than 300 in the provinces. Moreover, from the 1840s music-halls had been appearing, developing out of casual entertainment in drinking places. There were forty music-halls by 1900, mainly carrying on parts of the old 'illegitimate' tradition, but now with such new features as high-pressure publicity campaigns and fantastic salaries, and with some new and valuable developments in variety. The old market fairs declined in importance, but the menagerie and the 'horse-riding' developed, by the last quarter of the nineteenth century, into the circus. In the same period, football and racing became parts of organized entertainment, with regular meetings, charges for admission, and many more spectators.

In the 1890s a further series of changes began to appear. In 1896 the first wireless patent was registered and the first cinema show in England took place, later transferring to run in a music-hall. The full effect of the wireless and the cinema did not become apparent until the 1920s, but meanwhile there were very important changes in the organization of the Press. The 'Northcliffe Revolution', as it is usually called, was not the invention of popular journalism; this had begun as early as the Sunday papers of the 1830s and perhaps before. The crucial change made by Northcliffe was in the economic organization of the Press.

Throughout the eighteenth and nineteenth centuries the newspapers had relied, to varying degrees, on some income from advertising. This was at its highest point of importance in the mid-eighteenth century, and at its lowest in the second half of the nineteenth century. Such advertisement was mainly of the kind we now call 'classified': specific individual notices. But, outside the Press, other kinds of advertising had been rapidly developing. In its early days it was closely connected with fairs and in particular with the travellers selling patent medicines. Their methods got into print, partly through the newspapers, but more commonly through bills and posters. In the early and middle years of the nineteenth century billposting became a large and organized trade. All kinds of buildings were used, often without consent, and eventually in 1862 special hoardings were organized by the Billposters' Association. Handbills were still given out in extraordinary numbers in the streets, and men and vehicles were hired to parade boards and displays. These became so many that in 1853 the men were officially confined to the gutters and the vehicles were forbidden. New developments followed: skyline and balloon advertisements, larger posters on the new hoardings, electric signs. At last, from the 1880s, the new kinds of display advertising began to break into the Press, at a time when changes in marketing and the development of the retail trade were altering the whole basis of advertising. Northcliffe and similar figures saw increased revenue from the new display advertising as the key to modern newspaper finance, and in particular as a means to reduction in price per copy so as to gain a large circulation. He published his own circulation figures, and challenged his rivals to do the same. The new-style advertising agencies supported this challenge, which was not finally successful until 1931. By this time the whole structure of the nineteenth-century Press had been radically altered. The typical nineteenth-century newspaper, while using advertising revenue, was in no way dependent on it. The typical twentieth-century newspaper became heavily dependent on advertising revenue to the extent of just under a half of all revenue in the popular newspapers, and some three-quarters of all revenue in the traditional minority newspapers. If, in these different classes of advertising, sufficient revenue could not be obtained, the typical commercial newspaper was now closed down.

A second part of this major reorganization was the development of groups or chains of newspapers and magazines. The typical form of ownership in the nineteenth century had been by a printer, a printing family, or a small company. It was rare for more than one paper to be owned by the same person or company. But the new kind of owner, such as Northcliffe, Pearson, and Newnes, built up groups of magazines and then went on to start or acquire newspapers. This process has continued all through this century, and newspapers and magazines have nearly all passed from their previous status as independent private enterprises to membership of these new kinds of capitalist combine.

In recent years this process has been accelerating. There seem certain to be further changes, but in 1974 eighty-four per cent of all national morning papers sold were controlled by four groups (Reed International-IPC, News International, Beaverbrook Newspapers and Associated Newspapers), while eighty-six per cent of all national Sunday papers sold were controlled by three of these same groups (Reed International-IPC, News International and Beaverbrook Newspapers). The two London evening papers were controlled by two of the four dominant groups in national morning papers (Beaverbrook Newspapers and Associated Newspapers). A significant part of the provincial press is owned by groups including three of those mentioned –

Associated Newspapers, News International and Reed International-IPC – together with a fourth, Thomson (owner of Times Newspapers), and the large Westminster Press Group. Reed International-IPC, which controls thirty-five per cent of all national morning and Sunday papers sold, has also a majority ownership of large-circulation women's magazines, and is a very large owner of periodicals of all kinds.

The expansion of readership in this century has been great. By 1920 one adult in two read a daily paper, while every four adults read five Sunday papers. By 1947 every ten adults read twelve daily papers and twenty-three Sunday papers. The total circulation of national daily papers was 9,943,000 in 1937; 15,563,000 in 1947; 15,812,000 in 1961; 14,948,000 in 1968 and 15,433,000 in 1974. The total circulation of national Sunday papers was 13,315,000 in 1937; 25,239,000 in 1947; 24,536,000 in 1961; 24,177,000 in 1968 and 22,641,000 in 1974. In general a plateau was reached in the years immediately after 1945; there has since been some slight though uneven decline, still at very high overall levels. At the same time the range of papers available has steadily declined. Where there were nine evening papers in the London area at the end of the nineteenth century there are now (and precariously) only two. Seven national daily or Sunday papers have been closed since the beginning of 1960. By comparison with 1900 there is a vastly expanded total readership and a seriously limited range of choice. The papers which have been recently closed usually had substantial circulations; even very large circulations by all earlier standards, and by contemporary standards in most other, even larger societies. The last available figures for five of the seven national papers which were closed show sales of over two million (*Empire News*), one and a half million (*Dispatch*), and over one million each (*News Chronicle*, *Graphic*,

Sunday Chronicle), while the two most recent closures (since the last edition of this book; further closures may overtake the present edition) had sales of over three quarters of a million (*Sketch*) and nearly a quarter of a million (*Citizen*, formerly *Reynolds' News*). Such figures show that it cannot reasonably be said that these papers had to close because people would not buy them. It is simply that, in modern British Press finance, such high actual figures are not high enough to attract the necessary amounts of advertising revenue. Papers with much lower circulations, such as *The Times* and the *Guardian* (about four hundred thousand each), survive because the nature of their readership (people with higher incomes and more social influence) enables them to get advertising revenue at higher rates. So the position is that newspapers do not survive or fail according to how many people want them, but according to their suitability as media for advertising. This is a distinctive feature of this large part of communications in twentieth-century Britain.

The theatre has been steadily declining in the same period. The 400 theatres and music-halls in the country in 1900 have declined to some 200, and the decline is continuing. An important part of this decline is due to competition from cinemas, which created in their turn a new and very large audience. By 1939, the cinema audience in Britain was nineteen million people a week, and by 1946 over thirty-one million. Since the end of the war there has been a decline, rapidly accelerated by the coming of television. By 1955 the weekly audience was down to twenty-two million, by 1965 to six million and by 1974 to under three million. During this post-war decline, more than two thirds of all cinemas have been closed. In 1950 there were 4,584 cinemas open; in 1960 some 3,034 and in 1974 some 1,200 with internal alterations to provide 1,600 screens.

The expansion of the theatre in the nineteenth century,

and of the cinema in the twentieth century, show certain common features. In the early phase, in each case, typical ownership was by a small speculator, who gradually built up a local group. In later phases, combines similar to those which emerged in the Press began to be established, especially in the London theatre, in chains of provincial halls, and in the large cinema circuits. In the cinema there has been closely interlocking ownership of both the distributing and the production sides. In decline, both theatres and cinemas have been treated as ordinary commercial property, and have often been closed as part of speculative property schemes.

The characteristic form of ownership of the means of communication in twentieth-century Britain was set aside when broadcasting began to be developed. Perhaps because of its implications for national security, the early development of broadcasting was soon taken over by a public authority from the original trade combine. In 1927 a Royal Charter established the B.B.C. as an independent public corporation, with monopoly rights. This charter was renewed in 1937, and then covered the early development of television. The first public television service had been established by the B.B.C. in 1936. In 1954, the television monopoly was broken, and a second authority, I.T.A., set up by Act of Parliament. The Independent Television Authority (now, with the addition of commercial radio stations, the Independent Broadcasting Authority) owns its means of transmission, but contracts for the provision of programmes with some thirteen companies. Where the B.B.C. draws its revenue from a proportion of receiving licence fees, the I.B.A. is maintained by payments from the programme companies, which obtain their own revenue from selling advertising time. Thus, by the middle nineteen-fifties, a form very similar to that which had emerged in the Press could be discerned in what became the majority television service. A major part of revenue is derived from advertising, on which the programme companies, like newspapers, are dependent. The element of control by I.B.A., and by the terms of the Act establishing it, is a differentiating factor. It is significant, in terms of the general situation, that much of the investment in the programme companies has been by the existing newspaper combines, and by similar groups in the theatre and cinema. There has been a successful recent campaign to extend this system, with its dependence on advertising revenue, to sound broadcasting by local commercial stations.

The growth of audiences for broadcasting has been spectacular. Between twenty and twenty-five million people watch television every day. The great majority of families have one or more radio sets and ninety-six per cent of the population have television in their homes. Audiences for particular programmes are the largest ever known in the history of our communications. Broadcasting, together with the development of recording, has led to an extraordinary increase in audiences for music of all kinds. Nearly two hundred million records a year are being sold in the mid-seventies.

In books, also, there has been a major expansion. By 1901 the number of annual titles had reached 6,000. By 1924 it was over 12,000; by 1937 over 17,000; by 1963 over 26,000 and by 1973 over 35,000, of which more than 25,000 were new titles. Library facilities have been greatly expanded, and in the mid-seventies there are some six hundred million loans annually in the Public Library service (a very high figure by comparison with most other societies, and one which affects comparative book *sales* in Britain, which in hardbacks especially are relatively low). Since the mid-1930s there has been a remarkable expansion in paperback production: in the mid-1950s sales were some twenty million a year; in the mid-1960s some eighty million and in the mid-1970s some one hundred and seventy million. The actual book-reading public, and the much smaller book-buying public, are difficult to quantify, but the book-reading public is probably about sixty per cent of the population (of course with great unevenness as to actual use). This majority public for books was probably first achieved in the 1950s, by comparison with a majority public for Sunday papers by 1910 and for daily papers by the end of the First World War.

The production of books is undergoing similar changes of ownership to those noted for the Press at the end of the nineteenth century. There are still some independent publishers, but there is also a marked and accelerating tendency towards combine ownership, and already a considerable number of apparently independent imprints have been absorbed into large publishing groups.

What can we learn from this general record? It is clear that there are two major factors in the modern history of communications. There is, first, the remarkable expansion of audiences. In newspapers, magazines, books, broadcasting, television, and recorded music there has been an expansion beyond any previous conception, and this is still continuing. The recent decline in the cinema audience still leaves a very large public, and the decline in the theatre can be offset by this expansion, and especially by the great increase in audiences for drama through broadcasting and television. The whole process has the effect of a cultural revolution.

At the same time, there has been another major development. The ownership of the means of communication, old and new, has passed or is passing, in large part, to a kind of financial organization unknown in earlier periods, and with important resemblances to the major forms of ownership in general industrial production. The methods and attitudes of capitalist business have established themselves at the centre of public communications. There is the widespread dependence on advertising money, which leads to a policy of getting a large audience as quickly as possible, to attract and hold advertisers. From this it becomes one of the major purposes of communication – in most cases, the overriding purpose – to sell a particular paper or programme. All the basic purposes of communication – the sharing of human experience – are being steadily subordinated to this drive to sell.

The pressure here has been increasing. The old kind of newspaper proprietor, who wanted control so that he could propagate his opinions, has, in general, been replaced by a kind of proprietor who says he is not interested in opinions but simply in selling as many papers as he can. What was once a means to some larger policy has become in most cases the policy itself. The organization of communications is then not for use, but for profit, and we have passed the stage in which there has to be any pretence that things are otherwise.

This emphasis inevitably extends into the substance of communication. It is bound to remain a human world, in some form; it can never be only the production of things. But methods learned from the selling of things can be applied to persons. There can be a kind of manufacture and marketing of personalities, as in the powerful and expanding world of publicity. There can also be a kind of packaging of experience: putting it out with the right gloss, or even making the gloss a substitute for the experience. The human effects of such tendencies are bound to be serious, but attention to them can be dismissed as 'idealism' while the emphasis on selling is seen as normal and practical. The irony is that the only practical use of communication is the sharing of real experience. To set anything above this is in fact quite unpractical. To set selling above it may seem normal, but is really only a perversion to which some people have got used: a way of looking at the world which must be right and normal because you have cut yourself down to its size.

The interaction between these two major processes – the popular expansion and the emphasis on selling – is extremely complicated. The two are tied together in our minds, because they happened together. It is difficult to see that things might have been otherwise, can still be otherwise.

The correct historical analysis is twofold. First, it is clear that the extension of communications has been part of the extension of democracy. Yet, in this century, while the public has extended, ownership and control of the means of communication have narrowed. There is fear of public control because of the memories of State control in the past, but control can be of many kinds. In the modern combine system there is a new kind of control, and we might agree with Burke that

Wise men will apply their remedies to vices, not to names . . . Otherwise you will be wise historically, a fool in practice . . . You are terrifying yourself with ghosts and apparitions, whilst your house is the haunt of robbers.

In the modern trend towards limited ownership, the cultural conditions of democracy are in fact being denied: sometimes, ironically, in the name of freedom.

Second, it is clear that the expansion has been and is a process of human growth. All growth is difficult, and needs time and care. Many kinds of confusion and uncertainty are inevitably encountered. If the attempt is made to preserve old forms intact, and to denounce the new in their name, the old forms simply become irrelevant to the new problems. What can then happen is that control of the new forms passes to men who are not interested in the growth of the society, or in the human purposes the expansion is serving. Such men will see inexperience as an opportunity, and confusion as a sanction. Instead of a new culture emerging, a synthetic culture – meeting and exploiting the tensions of growth – will be devised for a quick sale. While such men rule, there will indeed be expansion but there will be no real growth.

A synthetic culture is easy. An old culture is remote. We are caught in this tension, yet the forces of growth, the real drives of the expansion, cannot in the end be denied. Already, through many difficulties, there has been growth of a real and valuable kind. But the nature of the expansion warns us that we cannot apply any simple overall test. We have to recognize the contradictions we have been following: between democracy and limited ownership: between genuine extension and the drive to sell. The real history of communications, in showing us the contradictions, shows us also the need to choose between genuinely alternative directions for the future.

CHAPTER THREE

CONTENT

WE get used to particular papers and programmes and often, after a while, come to take their typical content for granted. Some degree of familiarity with a particular paper or programme is indeed often necessary, if what it has to offer is to come through to us easily. But of course there is a danger, as we get used to the particular way of looking at the world which our favourite paper or programme embodies, that we shall forget that it is, after all, only one of many possible ways. Most of us realize that the worlds seen by *The Times* and by the *Daily Mirror*, or by Radio Three and Radio One, are in certain basic ways different. But to know only these general and obvious differences is not enough. If we are to be really alert and independent, as in a democracy we need to be, we have to look critically at the content and methods we are used to as well as those which we have decided are not our kind. There are several ways in which we can make this examination for ourselves. I want to illustrate some of them, both to show possible methods and to give some actual material. This kind of examination needs to be carried out regularly, not only so that we can keep in touch with important changes (which are often not announced), but also so that we can make historical comparisons and discern particular trends. Also, there is always some error in sampling, and this can only be reduced if other samples are taken and if many people are carrying out the examination. Where similar work has been done previously, I have kept as far as possible to procedures which allow comparisons. But such work has been scattered and irregular, and I have tried to introduce some new kinds. I will set this work out in three sections: first, measurement by categories of content; second, analysis of style and presentation; third, comparative survey.

MEASUREMENT BY CATEGORIES

Here I propose to look at a sample of newspapers, magazines, and programmes, in terms of the proportions of space and time given to different categories of material. I begin with the Press, and with national morning newspapers in particular. I want to look first at the division of available space into advertising and all other (editorial) material. Table 1 sets out

Table 1(a)

July 1961	Price in pence	Pages	Average circulation in thousands	Percentage editorial material	Percentage advertising material
Times	5	18	260	68	32
Guardian	4	16	235	61	39
Telegraph	3	22	1,264	52	48
Mail	3	16	2,687	68	32
Express	3	12	4,313	66	34
Herald†	3	10	1,418	77	23
Worker‡	3	4	?	97	3
Mirror	3	20*	4,593	67	33
Sketch	3	16*	1,000	90	10

* Tabloid size.
† Now succeeded by the *Sun*.
‡ Now succeeded by the *Morning Star*.

the results of a sample analysis; the price, number of pages, and average circulation of the papers are included to see what relation they may have to the advertising and editorial figures.

The division of space between advertising and editorial material is not, then, governed by whether a paper is

'quality' or 'popular'. The three papers with the lowest proportions of advertising, the *Herald*, *Sketch*, and *Worker*, would
certainly have included more if they could have got it. The
Herald and *Sketch* got less because by comparison with their
immediate competitors their circulations were low. *The Times*
and *Guardian*, with lower circulations, got relatively more advertising because the social and economic standing of their
readers attracted advertisers. The *Worker* got very little advertising because of its political policy combined with its
small circulation. When these exceptions are allowed for, we
get an average figure of roughly one third of all available
space being given to advertising.

Further sample analyses, for comparison and continuity,
were made in 1965 and in 1973.

Table 1(b)

July 1965	Price in pence	Pages	Average circulation in thousands	Percentage editorial material	Percentage advertising material
Times	6	24	258	64	36
Guardian	5	22	276	63	37
Telegraph	4	32	1,351	44	56
Mail	3	16	2,425	61	39
Express	4	16	4,042	61	39
Sun†	4	14	1,361	69	31
Worker‡	4	4	60	96	4
Mirror	4	24*	4,957	65	35
Sketch	4	20*	826	80	20

* Tabloid size.
† Successor to *Herald*.
‡ Now succeeded by the *Morning Star*.

One significant feature of these tables is some overall
decline of circulation; there has also, of course, been a significant rise in selling prices. Within the general movement of
circulations it is notable that *The Times*, *Guardian* and *Tele-*

graph have gone up, and the *Mirror*, *Express* and *Mail* gone down. But this is not a simple move from the 'popular' to the 'quality' press. The remarkable increase for the *Sun*, under its new management, has been an increase in the popularity of an older style of popular pictorial journalism, sharing hardly any of the relative movements towards serious journalism evident elsewhere.

Table 1(c)

July 1973	Price in new pence*	Pages	Average circulation in thousands	Percentage editorial material	Percentage advertising material
Times	5 (12)	32	344	62	38
Guardian	5 (12)	24	345	73	27
Telegraph	4 (9·6)	36	1,419	48	52
Mail	3 (7·2)	40†	1,729	60	40
Express	3 (7·2)	20	3,290	60	40
Sun	3 (7·2)	32†	2,966	64	36
Star‡	4 (9·6)	6	?	91	9
Mirror	3 (7·2)	28†	4,291	63	37

* Price in old pence in brackets.
† Tabloid size.
‡ Formerly *Worker*.

The dependence on advertising has increased during the period. The average percentage for all papers in 1961 was 28 (excluding the *Worker* the percentage was 31). By 1965 these percentages had increased respectively to 33 and 36, and by 1973 to 35 and 39. The weakness of the *Sketch*, in advertising percentage, was a main factor in its closure.

The dependence of newspapers on a substantial proportion of advertising has been normal since the period between the wars. If we look at the percentage of advertising space in three typical papers over a period, we find:

	1937	1955	1961	1965	1973
Times	33	40	32	36	38
Mail	41	36	32	39	40
Mirror	26	34	33	35	37

Whether the paper is, in conventional terms, 'quality', 'popular' or 'tabloid', a comparable dependence on commercial advertising can be seen, in our period, to be a common characteristic.

However, advertising is a very general category. If we look at the use of advertising space, we find some important differences between kinds of paper. For example, some papers have a high proportion of classified advertisements (specific notices, usually in ordinary size type); others a high proportion of display advertisements (usually very general and persuasive in tone, using illustrations and often very large type). In Table 2 (p. 34) there are some sample percentages. We can usually spot these marked differences simply by looking at the papers concerned. But there are other differences in the use of advertising space which have to be more carefully examined. It is worth picking out certain classes of goods and services, to see what proportions of space they get in different papers. A sample distribution is shown in Table 3 (pp. 35–6).

This is the distribution of *display* advertising only, leaving aside the different proportions of classified and display already noted. Obviously there are variations in these percentages, from time to time, but some general points are very clear. Most important, perhaps, is the category described as 'inter-company and public opinion' advertising, which on its present scale is a comparatively new development. Such advertisements aim at no direct or (for most people) conceivable buying. The products they advertise could only be bought by quite large organizations, and often only by quite specialized trades. Why then advertise in a general newspaper rather than a trade periodical? The usual explanation is that the newspapers actually used for this kind of advertising have among their readers the highest proportions of people in a position to make such large buying decisions, and this is obviously true so far as it goes. Yet such proportions must be quite small, by comparison with the actual proportions of space. The explanation seems to be that, quite apart from any actual business promoted by these advertisements, the prestige or 'image' of the company is promoted among readers held to be particularly influential in leading public opinion. In bulk, such advertising seems also to promote the 'image' of modern business as a whole. The borderline between this and straight political advertising is often quite difficult to see.

The distribution of display advertising forms a reasonably clear pattern. The more expensive goods and services, notably travel and cars, were in 1961 heavily advertised in the more expensive papers, or those reaching readers with most money. By 1973, for general social reasons, this was much less true, especially for cars. Distribution of the middle range of display advertising is less significant: the local variations in these particular samples are not particularly important, and further sampling would undoubtedly amend them. But just as the significant feature of display in the more expensive papers is the crucial 'inter-company and public opinion' category, so one significant and continuing feature of display in the cheaper range is the distribution of patent medicine advertising, which seems to be concentrated in the papers reaching the poorest and least educated members of the community. This apparently conscious policy needs the most careful and continuing observation. One significant new tendency is shown by a new category – 'Personal Financial' – in Table 3 (c). This relates to the intensive development, during the sixties and early seventies, of a new kind of selling of capitalist stock, in 'unit trusts' and similar devices, and of building society shares, to a wider public. We shall see that this is directly reflected in an increase of 'financial news' of the same type.

Table 2(a)

July 1961	Times	Guardian	Telegraph	Mail	Express	Herald	Worker	Mirror	Sketch
Classified	69	66	85	12	13	27	34	9	19
Display	31	34	15	88	87	73	66	91	81

Table 2(b)

July 1965	Times	Guardian	Telegraph	Mail	Express	Sun	Worker	Mirror	Sketch
Classified	77	75	73	44	22	18	100	9	41
Display	23	25	27	56	78	82	0	91	59

Table 2(c)

July 1973	Times	Guardian	Telegraph	Mail	Express	Sun	Star	Mirror
Classified	67	$41\frac{1}{2}$	$67\frac{1}{2}$	37	$37\frac{1}{2}$	$34\frac{1}{2}$	100	$36\frac{1}{2}$
Display	33	$58\frac{1}{2}$	$32\frac{1}{2}$	63	$62\frac{1}{2}$	$65\frac{1}{2}$	0	$63\frac{1}{2}$

It will be seen from the period variations in Table 2 that there has been an important increase in classified advertising in the large-circulation papers and some increase in display advertising in the small-circulation papers. These trends make the contrast of distribution of types of advertising, between the two groups, less marked in 1973 than in 1961, though the contrast is still clearly there.

Table 3(a)

July 1961	Inter-company and public opinion	Travel	Cars	Drink and tobacco	Other consumer goods	Food	Patent medicines	Miscellaneous
Times	57	10	8	8	5	—	1	11
Guardian	48	7	8	9	18	—	1	9
Telegraph	37	9	8	6	28	1	8	3
Mail	—	2	2	13	55	10	9	9
Express	—	2	2	14	43	10	16	13
Herald	—	—	—	3	62	9	13	13
Worker	—	—	—	—	100	—	—	—
Mirror	—	—	—	13	59	9	16	3
Sketch	—	—	—	42	25	—	7	26

Table 3(b)

July 1965	Inter-company and public opinion	Travel	Cars	Drink and tobacco	Other consumer goods	Food	Patent medicines	Miscellaneous
Times	76	24	—	—	—	—	—	—
Guardian	63	14	11	—	12	—	—	—
Telegraph	54	8	14	7	9	8	—	—
Mail	—	—	7	31	20	37	2	3
Express	—	—	14	2	22	38	7	17
Sun	—	—	—	25	18	31	$\frac{1}{2}$	$25\frac{1}{2}$
Worker	—	—	—	—	—	—	—	—
Mirror	—	—	—	22	39	19	19	1
Sketch	—	8	—	14	8	42	24	4

Table 3(c)

July 1973	Inter-company and public opinion	Personal Financial	Travel	Cars	Drinks and Tobacco	Other consumer goods	Food	Patent medicines	Miscellaneous
Times	61	5	2	24	—	6½	—	—	1½
Guardian	80½	—	2	16½	1	—	—	—	—
Telegraph	41½	20½	10	20	—	4	—	—	4
Mail	—	57	—	11	12	9	5	5	1
Express	6½	24	8½	19	6½	13	10½	5	6
Sun	7	24	—	16½	14	2	25	5½	6
Star	—	—	—	—	—	—	—	—	—
Mirror	—	13	—	16	16	15	30	8	2

I have dealt so far only with the use of advertising space. I have done this because it is part of the content of a paper which can so easily be overlooked, although it is a very important part both in size and style. I turn now to the use of the remaining space, usually about two-thirds of the paper. There is a sample distribution of 1961 percentages in Table 4(a). The classification used in this table follows that in Appendix VII of the Report of the Royal Commission on the Press, 1947–9. The categories are self-explanatory, except for 'miscellaneous', which includes cartoons and puzzles. The differences between various papers stand out quite clearly. Most notable, perhaps, is the high proportion of cartoon and similar material, and the low proportion of news, in the two 'tabloid' papers, *Mirror* and *Sketch*. In proportions given to pictures, there are less differences now than there once were, when the term 'picture-paper' could indicate a distinct kind. A difference in use and kind of picture will be noted later.

It is worth noting that the proportion of news, in contem-

Table 4(a)

July 1961	News	Features	Leaders	Letters	Pictures	Miscellaneous
Times	74	8	3	2½	11	1½
Guardian	64	17	3	3	10	3
Telegraph	61	18	2	3	14	2
Mail	55	8½	1	1	25½	9
Express	62	8	1	1	18	10
Herald	64	9	2	2	14	9
Worker	70	12	3	1	12	2
Mirror	45	7	1	2	29	16
Sketch	49	7	1	2	18	23

porary newspapers, is not always very high. Indeed, if we take it as a proportion of the total material (including advertising) printed, the highest figure is that of the *Worker*, at some sixty-eight per cent (a misleading figure in some ways because of the very small amount of advertising included), while the other papers range from the fifty per cent of *The Times* to the thirty per cent of the *Mirror*. But we must bring to these figures a further analysis, if we are to assess content accurately. We must look at the proportions of total news space given to particular kinds of news. A sample distribution of 1961 percentages is given in Table 5(a).

The differences here are very interesting, and repay careful study. Here, especially, pictures of the world – selections of things worth attending to – are formed and communicated. We must not of course make the mistake of assuming that the only serious news is that classified as 'political, social, and economic'; there are many other kinds of human fact which can be serious news. Yet the Press is so often discussed in

Table 4(b)

July 1965	News	Features	Leaders	Letters	Pictures	Miscellaneous
Times	79	$7\frac{1}{2}$	$2\frac{1}{2}$	2	$7\frac{1}{2}$	2
Guardian	66	20	$2\frac{1}{2}$	$1\frac{1}{2}$	6	4
Telegraph	67	19	2	1	9	2
Mail	$63\frac{1}{2}$	13	1	$\frac{1}{2}$	10	12
Express	67	8	1	2	9	13
Sun	63	$12\frac{1}{2}$	$2\frac{1}{4}$	$2\frac{1}{4}$	10	10
Worker	67	13	3	—	10	7
Mirror	63	5	1	3	12	16
Sketch	51	$13\frac{1}{2}$	$1\frac{1}{2}$	1	18	15

Table 4(c)

July 1973	News	Features	Leaders	Letters	Pictures	Miscellaneous
Times	67	19	2	$4\frac{1}{2}$	$4\frac{1}{2}$	3
Guardian	68	21	2	2	4	3
Telegraph	$77\frac{1}{2}$	$7\frac{1}{2}$	$1\frac{1}{2}$	$1\frac{1}{2}$	$7\frac{1}{2}$	$4\frac{1}{2}$
Mail	$61\frac{1}{2}$	18	$1\frac{1}{2}$	5	8	6
Express	58	$19\frac{1}{2}$	1	—	$14\frac{1}{2}$	7
Sun	$58\frac{1}{2}$	8	$3\frac{1}{2}$	$2\frac{1}{2}$	20	$7\frac{1}{2}$
Star	$61\frac{1}{2}$	18	2	$\frac{1}{2}$	12	6
Mirror	$61\frac{1}{2}$	$10\frac{1}{2}$	$2\frac{1}{2}$	2	16	$7\frac{1}{2}$

terms of this one function, giving the facts necessary for political, social, and economic judgement in a democracy, that it is worth noting not only the differences between papers, but the actual proportions in any and all. If we take political, social and economic news, both international and domestic, as a proportion of the total material (including advertising) printed, the highest figure is the rather special case of the *Worker*, with thirty-nine per cent, while the other papers range from around sixteen per cent, for *The Times* and the *Guardian*, to the lowest figure of about five per cent in the *Sketch*. These are quite startling figures, by comparison with our usual assumptions about the main functions of our newspapers.

Table 5(a)

July 1961	International political, social and economic	Domestic political, social and economic	Law, police, and accidents	Personalities	Sport	Arts including radio and television	Financial and Commercial	Miscellaneous
Times	18	11	1	6	23	10	28	3
Guardian	21	19	1	1	28	12	15	3
Telegraph	21	14½	3½	5	34½	9	11	1½
Mail	9	12	12	8	35	8	9	7
Express	16	13	17	3	42	2	2	5
Herald	11	15	9	12	43	6	3	1
Worker	19	38	1	—	29	10	—	3
Mirror	5	13	14	17	38	2	—	11
Sketch	2	9	14	17	36	3	3	16

Later analyses, in 1965 and 1973, gave the following tables for comparison.

Table 5(b)

July 1965	International political, social and economic	Domestic political, social and economic	Law, police and accidents	Personalities	Sport	Arts including radio and television	Financial and Commercial	Miscellaneous
Times	13	$23\frac{1}{2}$	5	6	$15\frac{1}{2}$	$7\frac{1}{2}$	28	$1\frac{1}{2}$
Guardian	$19\frac{1}{2}$	31	$4\frac{1}{2}$	1	9	21	14	—
Telegraph	7	29	4	4	23	16	17	—
Mail	14	24	5	10	31	4	12	—
Express	4	$14\frac{1}{2}$	10	10	$52\frac{1}{2}$	2	7	—
Sun	$4\frac{1}{2}$	$33\frac{1}{2}$	$14\frac{1}{2}$	3	$32\frac{1}{2}$	2	9	1
Worker	8	47	4	—	34	7	—	—
Mirror	2	22	26	14	31	4	1	—
Sketch	2	19	13	15	49	1	1	—

Table 5(c)

July 1973	International political, social and economic	Domestic political, social and economic	Law, police and accidents	Personalities	Sport	Arts including radio and television	Medical and Scientific	Financial and Commercial	Miscellaneous
Times	17	30	2	3	17	2	1	28	—
Guardian	25	27	1	—	21	10	—	16	—
Telegraph	12	39	$\frac{1}{2}$	$1\frac{1}{2}$	$18\frac{1}{2}$	$2\frac{1}{2}$	—	26	—
Mail	5	27	—	7	32	$1\frac{1}{2}$	—	26	$1\frac{1}{2}$
Express	$9\frac{1}{2}$	21	2	$6\frac{1}{2}$	$46\frac{1}{2}$	$2\frac{1}{2}$	—	12	—
Sun	$1\frac{1}{2}$	39	$\frac{1}{2}$	$7\frac{1}{2}$	50	—	—	$1\frac{1}{2}$	—
Star	$11\frac{1}{2}$	55	—	—	30	$3\frac{1}{2}$	—	—	—
Mirror	$\frac{1}{4}$	34	—	14	$44\frac{1}{4}$	$2\frac{1}{4}$	—	$5\frac{1}{4}$	—

The most interesting changes to emerge from these later
figures are some increases in the amount of space given to
news, with some evident levelling between different kinds of
paper, and more recently an increase in features. By comparison with 1961 the amount of space given to pictures is
down, but this, after a decline in the mid-sixties, was rising
again in the later years, in the *Express*, the *Mirror* and especially the new-style *Sun*. These are, of course, changes in the
distribution of editorial matter only, and need to be seen
within the increase of advertising noted earlier. Thus, if we
take news as a proportion of the total material (including
advertising) printed, the highest figure is again that of the
Worker/Star (still a special case because of the very low proportion of advertising), while the other papers range from
about half (*The Times*, 1965, 49%; *Guardian*, 1973, 50%) to
rather more than a third (*Telegraph*, 1973, 37%; *Express*,
1973, 35%). Yet news, of course, is still of very variable
kinds. If we take political, social and economic news, both
international and domestic, as a proportion of the total
material (including advertising) printed, the highest figures
are again for the *Worker/Star* (1965, 35%; 1973, 66%), still
a special case. All the other papers show some increase in
this proportion in the later samples. The range in 1965 was
from twenty-three per cent in the *Guardian* to nine per cent in
the *Mirror* and seven per cent in the *Express*. The range in
1973 was from twenty-five per cent in the *Guardian* to eleven
per cent in the *Express*. Here again however we have to notice
significant differences in the proportions of news coverage of
international events. The 1965 sample showed a range of
international news as a percentage of all material (including
advertising) printed, from eight per cent in the *Guardian* to
less than one per cent in the *Sketch*. The 1973 sample showed a
range from twelve-and-a-half per cent in the *Guardian*,
through three-and-a-half per cent in the *Express*, to percent-

ages well below one per cent in the *Mirror* and the *Sun*. Here too, we might say, pictures of 'the world' are, by selection, relative emphasis and actual exclusion, decisively and perhaps disastrously formed.

A brief comparison of the space given to editorial and advertising material, and of the percentage of all space given to international and domestic political, social and economic news, can be made between the three English 'quality' papers and three directly comparable papers in France, West Germany and Italy.

Table 6

1965	Price	Pages	% Editorial	% Advertising	% Political, Social and Economic News
Times	6	24	64	36	19
Guardian	5	22	63	37	23
Telegraph	4	32	44	56	12
Le Monde	7†	24*	69	31	46
Die Welt	8†	22	51	49	33
La Stampa	6†	18	51	49	27

† Price to nearest penny, at normal exchange rate.
* Tabloid size.

We can turn next to the Sunday papers, for some comparative figures. In Table 7 there is a sample distribution between editorial and advertising space, with the relevant figures for price, size, and circulation.

The proportions of space given to advertising are generally rather higher in the Sunday papers. The one really low figure, for *Reynolds News* in 1961 and for its successor the *Sunday Citizen* in 1965, was related to low circulation and perhaps its political policy; by the late sixties the paper had been closed. The division of the percentage of space between classified and display advertising, given in Table 8, reveals a very similar pattern to that in the national morning Press, though there has been an increase in classified advertising in the more popular Sunday papers.

Table 7(a)

July 1961	Price in pence	Pages	Average circulation in thousands	Percentage editorial material	Percentage advertising material
S. Times	6	36	1,023	51	49
Observer	6	32	733	54	46
S. Telegraph	5	28	716	67	33
S. Express	5	28	3,767	51	49
People	5	18	5,442	60	40
News of World	5	16	6,734	67	33
Reynolds News	5	14	326	81	19
Pictorial	5	28*	5,335	70	30

*Tabloid size.

Table 7(b)

July 1965	Price in pence	Pages	Average circulation in thousands	Percentage editorial material	Percentage advertising material
S. Times	8	46+36*	1,275	47	53
Observer	7	32+32*	829	53	47
S. Telegraph	6	24	662	74	26
S. Express	6	24	4,187	55	45
People	6	20	5,509	60	40
News of World	6	18	6,175	65	35
S. Citizen	6	32*	236	84	16
S. Mirror	6	36*	5,022	66	34

* Tabloid size.

Table 7(c)

July 1973	Price in new pence*	Pages	Average circulation in thousands	Percentage editorial material	Percentage advertising material
S. Times	9 (21·6)	72+72†	1,516	39	61
Observer	8 (19·2)	40+48†	795	43	57
S. Telegraph	5 (12)	40	774	47	53
S. Express	5 (12)	32	4,096	46	54
People	5 (12)	22	4,423	45	55
News of World	5 (12)	24	5,943	50	50
S. Mirror	5 (12)	48†	4,543	57	43

* Price in old pence in brackets.
† Tabloid size.

Table 8(a)

July 1961	Sunday Times	Observer	Sunday Telegraph	Sunday Express	People	News of the World	Reynolds News	Sunday Pictorial
Classified	56	56	38	8	1	3	2	1
Display	44	44	62	92	99	97	98	99

Table 8(b)

July 1965	Sunday Times	Observer	Sunday Telegraph	Sunday Express	People	News of the World	Sunday Citizen	Sunday Mirror
Classified	63	61	68	23	21	20	20	12
Display	37	39	32	77	79	80	80	88

Table 8(c)

July 1973	Sunday Times	Observer	Sunday Telegraph	Sunday Express	People	News of the World	Sunday Mirror
Classified	46	56	44½	33	33	32	15
Display	54	44	55½	67	67	68	85

There are also important resemblances in the distribution of display advertising space for certain goods and services, as is shown by Table 9.

Table 9(a)

July 1961	Inter-company and public opinion	Travel	Cars	Drink and tobacco	Other consumer goods	Food	Patent medicines	Miscellaneous
Sunday Times	39	8	23	2	12	—	—	16
Observer	20	9	17	8	24	—	—	22
Sunday Telegraph	11	5	39	3	26	8	1	7
Sunday Express	6	4	24	12	35	1	3	15
People	6	3	6	14	31	6	14	20
News of the World	7	—	3	9	40	10	23	8
Reynolds News	13	—	14	3	15	41	2	12
Pictorial	—	1	6	18	52	7	9	7

Table 9(b)

July 1965	Inter-company and public opinion	Travel	Cars	Drink and tobacco	Other consumer goods	Food	Patent medicines	Miscellaneous
Sunday Times	22	7	7	14	29	3	2	16
Observer	13	15	14	20	17	—	—	21
Sunday Telegraph	—	16	26	—	12	17	3	26
Sunday Express	—	10	14	9	25	11	4	27
People	—	1	4	24	37	8	19	7
News of the World	—	1	29	14	27	—	16	13
Sunday Citizen	—	3	—	—	40	42	13	2
Sunday Mirror	—	4	2	15	41	2	12	24

Table 9(c)

July 1973	Inter-company and public opinion	Personal financial	Travel	Cars	Drink and tobacco	Other consumer goods	Food	Patent medicines	Miscellaneous
Sunday Times	28	35	5	9	3	10	—	—	10
Observer	16	29½	6½	16½	9	14½	—	2½	5½
Sunday Telegraph	—	75½	5	13	—	2½	—	1	3
Sunday Express	—	23	15	19	—	24	8	2	9
People	—	11½	5½	—	5½	27	7	7	36½
News of the World	4	9	6	4	12	23	8	12	22
Sunday Mirror	—	22½	1½	8½	7	20½	11½	7	21½

Here the importance of inter-company and public opinion advertising, in certain papers, is again clear, as is also the concentration of patent medicine advertising and the increase in personal financial advertising. The distribution of other display advertising follows the now characteristic pattern.

When we turn to the use of editorial space, we find important differences. A sample distribution of percentages is given in Table 10(a).

Table 10(a)

July 1961	News	Features	Leaders	Letters	Pictures	Miscellaneous
Sunday Times	50	24	5	3	14	4
Observer	49	25	5	3	11	7
Sunday Telegraph	55	22	3	2	14	4
Sunday Express	40	30	1	1	20	8
People	52	23	2	2	13	8
News of the World	67	12	1	1	6	13
Reynolds News	50	28	2	3	14	3
Pictorial	50	18	1	1	24	6

It is now an established feature of the Sunday Press that it gives more of its space to features of all kinds, and correspondingly less to news, than the national morning papers.

Only the *News of the World* prints as large a proportion of news as most of the morning papers, and this is rather a special case. We can only interpret these figures adequately if we analyse kinds of news. A sample distribution of percentages is set out in Table 11(a).

It will be seen that whereas news of law cases, police investigations, and accidents exceeded international and domestic political, social, and economic news in only one

Table 11(a)

July 1961	International political, social and economic	Domestic political, social and economic	Law, police, and accidents	Personalities	Sport	Arts	Financial and commercial	Miscellaneous
Sunday Times	10	7	1	9	28	30	12	3
Observer	15	17	1	6	22	35	4	—
Sunday Telegraph	12	9	2	3	31	28	12	3
Sunday Express	8	4	11	11	35	2	11	18
People	1	4	38	4	45	2	—	6
News of the World	9	5	36	5	39	1	3	2
Reynolds News	11	10	8	6	40	17	2	6
Pictorial	4	7	13	11	51	4	—	10

national morning paper, there was an excess of this kind in
three Sunday papers, and in two of them – the *People* and the
News of the World – it was very marked. Sports news exceeded
political, social, and economic news in five out of nine morning papers; in Sunday papers it did so in all but one case. The
share of space given to all political, social, and economic
news, in the total material (including advertising) printed,
varied from the highest figures of between eight per cent and
nine per cent in the *Observer* and *Reynolds News* to the lowest of
under two per cent in the *People*. There was an even wider
variation in the share of space given to news of the arts (books,
films, plays, television, radio, music, etc.), from 9·5 per cent
in the *Observer* to between 0·4 per cent and 0·5 per cent in the
Sunday Express and the *News of the World*.

Later sample analyses were made, for comparison and
continuity.

Table 10(b)

July 1965	News	Features	Leaders	Letters	Pictures	Miscellaneous
Sunday Times	46	25	1	2	23	3
Observer	39	20	2	2	29	8
Sunday Telegraph	63	19	1	2	10	5
Sunday Express	52	23	1	2	13	9
People	61	20	1	4	11	3
News of the World	60	14	1	1	14	10
Sunday Citizen	46	12	1	4	16	21
Sunday Mirror	47	25	—	3	23	2

Table 10(c)

July 1973	News	Features	Leaders	Letters	Pictures	Miscellaneous
Sunday Times	32½	36½	½	1½	26½	2½
Observer	45	31½	½	2	18	3
Sunday Telegraph	57	29½	1	2½	7½	2½
Sunday Express	50	26	—	2½	18	3½
People	54	13	1	5½	17½	9
News of the World	49	27½	1	4	14	4½
Sunday Mirror	41½	16½	1½	2	30½	8

The generally low figures for news, by comparison with the morning papers, are confirmed in these later analyses, with minor shifts between papers. The most striking change in the editorial content of the Sunday papers is in the colour supplements of the *Sunday Times* and *Observer*, which had the effect of markedly raising the proportion of space given to pictures.

It is noticeable that the advertising photographs and the editorial photographs, in these colour supplements, are very similar in kind and style, to the point where it can require close inspection to distinguish between them at all. By no means all editorial photographs, in the Sunday papers generally, are news photographs, as a look at the *News of the World* or the *Sunday Mirror*, among others, will show. But it is in the colour supplements that a new editorial method is evident, the feature photographs combining with the advertising photographs to present an overall style, evidently intended to suggest what might be called (with an effort) a way of life. This combination of advertising and feature techniques was new only in the sense that it was now, for the first time in this form, entering newspapers. It had been familiar for some years in the women's magazines, from which, as a journalistic method, the colour supplements evidently derive.

In the distribution of editorial attention, some interesting changes may be seen in Tables 11(b) and (c).

Table 11(b)

July 1965	International political, social and economic	Domestic political, social and economic	Law, police, and accidents	Personalities	Sport	Arts	Financial and commercial	Miscellaneous
Sunday Times	13	10	2	6	21	20	25	3
Observer	14	15	1	7	27	25	9	2
Sunday Telegraph	10	17	3	1	31	16	20	2
Sunday Express	11	19	6	10	37	3	10	4
People	1	33	4	14	38	4	1	5
News of the World	2	10	32	13	38	2	2	1
Sunday Citizen	7	31	2	16	32	9	2	1
Sunday Mirror	12	23	7	6	40	1	4	7

Table 11(c)

July 1973	International political, social and economic	Domestic political, social and economic	Law, police and accidents	Personalities	Sport	Arts	Medical and scientific	Financial and commercial	Miscellaneous
Sunday Times	10	13	—	—	26½	12	2½	36	—
Observer	17	15	—	—	22	25	1	17	3
Sunday Telegraph	9	14	—	1	25	20	1	30	—
Sunday Express	10½	16	—	10½	40	6½	5½	9½	1½
People	1½	25	26½	—	45½	—	—	1½	—
News of the World	—	7	30	6½	51½	5	—	—	—
Sunday Mirror	2	16	4	20	45	7	2	4	—

In the 1965 sample, news of law cases, police investigations and accidents exceeded international and domestic political, social and economic news in only one Sunday paper, as it also did in only one morning paper. In the 1973 sample there was only one excess. In 1965 sports news exceeded political, social and economic news in three out of nine morning papers, and in five out of eight Sunday papers. In 1973 this excess occurred in three out of eight morning papers and in five out of seven Sundays. The share of space given to all news, in Sunday papers, in the total material (including advertising) printed varied in 1965 from forty-five per cent in the *Telegraph* to twenty-one per cent in the *Sunday Times* and *Observer*. In 1973 the range was lower, from twenty-seven per cent in the *Telegraph* to thirteen per cent in the *Sunday Times*. The share of space given to all political, social and economic news, in the total material printed, ranged in 1965 from the sixteen per cent of the *Citizen* (a special case because of its low advertising content) and then from twelve per cent in the *Telegraph* and *People* to six per cent in the *Observer* and five per cent in the *Sunday Times* and *News of the World*. In 1973 the range was rather higher, from fourteen per cent in the *Observer* to seven per cent in the *Mirror*. In both samples the range of news of the arts was from six per cent in the *Observer* to nought in the *News of the World*. But the share of space given to financial and commercial news has markedly risen. This category is distinguished from international or domestic economic news by its particular emphasis, which is news of companies and share prices as a guide to private investments, rather than news and analysis of a general kind, in these fields. In two papers in 1965 and three in 1973, this financial and commercial news exceeded all international political, social and economic news, and in one case in 1965 and in two in 1973 both international and domestic political, social and economic news. The pictures of the world, of issues requiring attention, that have been formed here are of great characteristic interest. The low quantity of international news is as marked in the Sundays as in the morning papers. The proportional range in 1965 was from some eight per cent in the *Sunday Telegraph* to less than one per cent in *The People* and the *News of the World*, and in 1973 from seven and a half per cent in the *Observer* to nought in the *News of the World*.

We can complete this account of the use of space in news-

Table 12(a)

July 1961	Price in pence	Pages	Average circulation in thousands	Percentage editorial material	Percentage advertising material	Classified as percentage of advertising	Display as percentage of advertising
News	3	16	1,486	51	49	58	42
Standard	3	28*	761	48	52	59	41

*Tabloid size.

papers by looking briefly at the two surviving London evening papers. Tables 12, 13, and 14 are set out for comparison.

Table 12(b)

July 1965	Price in pence	Pages	Average circulation in thousands	Percentage editorial material	Percentage advertising material	Classified as percentage of advertising	Display as percentage of advertising
News	4	18	1,278	37	63	77	23
Standard	4	32*	680	46	54	76	24

* Tabloid size.

Table 12(c)

July 1973	Price in new pence*	Pages	Average circulation in thousands	Percentage editorial material	Percentage advertising material	Classified as percentage of advertising	Display as percentage of advertising
News	3 (7·2)	24	834	39	61	61½	38½
Standard	3 (7·2)	56†	512	38½	61½	75	25

* Prices in old pence in brackets.
† Tabloid size.

Table 13(a)

July 1961	News	Features	Leaders	Letters	Pictures	Misc.
News	59	13	1	1	14	12
Standard	61½	11	1	1	15½	10

Table 13(b)

July 1965	News	Features	Leaders	Letters	Pictures	Misc.
News	58½	15½	1	1	13	11
Standard	61	14	1	2	12	10

Table 13(c)

July 1973	News	Features	Leaders	Letters	Pictures	Misc.
News	56	19	$\frac{1}{2}$	1	13	$10\frac{1}{2}$
Standard	$56\frac{1}{2}$	16	—	2	$18\frac{1}{2}$	7

Table 14(a)

July 1961	International political, social and economic	Domestic political, social and economic	Law, police and accidents	Personalities	Sport	Arts	Financial and commercial	Miscellaneous
News	1	18	11	9	36	3	16	6
Standard	$3\frac{1}{2}$	18	8	12	29	3	24	$2\frac{1}{2}$

Table 14(b)

July 1965	International political, social and economic	Domestic political, social and economic	Law, police and accidents	Personalities	Sport	Arts	Financial and commercial	Miscellaneous
News	1	11	7	19	20	12	18	12
Standard	5	18	15	8	31	3	13	7

Table 14(c)

July 1973	International political, social and economic	Domestic political, social and economic	Law, police and accidents	Personalities	Sport	Arts	Medical and Scientific	Financial and Commercial	Miscellaneous
News	1	32	10	12	24	$7\frac{1}{2}$	$\frac{1}{2}$	13	—
Standard	14	$19\frac{1}{2}$	9	8	28	3	2	$16\frac{1}{2}$	—

The magazines specially published for women and girls are now very important in forming pictures of the world. In most of them the content of advertising is high (see Table 15).

Table 15(a)

July 1961	Price in pence	Published	Pages	Percentage editorial material	Percentage advertising material
Woman's Own	6	weekly	76	52	48
Woman's Mirror	6	weekly	48	68	32
She	15	monthly	80	58	42
Vogue	30	monthly	110	54	46
Honey*	18	monthly	68	68	32
Boyfriend*	5	weekly	28	89	11

Table 15(b)

July 1965	Price in pence	Published	Pages	Percentage editorial material	Percentage advertising material
Woman's Own	8	weekly	60	59	41
Woman's Mirror	6	weekly	48	70	30
She	24	monthly	100	63	37
Vogue	36	monthly	108	62	38
Honey*	24	monthly	68	54	46
Boyfriend*	9	weekly	32	83	17

Table 15(c)

July 1973	Price in new pence	Published	Pages	Percentage editorial material	Percentage advertising material
Woman's Own	6	weekly	64	62	38
Vogue	30	monthly	152	50	50
Honey*	17½	monthly	140	41	59
Nova†	25	monthly	100	63	37

* Mainly for adolescent girls.
† Included as an example of a new type.

The magazines named are examples of each of the main types. Magazines marked* are mainly for adolescent girls. It is often not easy to separate advertising from editorial material. It is not only that the styles of presentation in each are remarkably similar. It is also that a good deal of more or less direct advertising is normally included in certain editorial features. Analysis of content is also not easy. All the magazines are extensively illustrated, with a familiar overlap of visual style between advertising and editorial material. Percentages of editorial photographs and drawings ranged, in *Woman's Own*, from forty-two per cent in 1965 to twenty-seven per cent in 1973; in *Vogue* from seventy-five per cent in 1965 to fifty-seven per cent in 1973; in *Honey* from fifty-one per cent in 1965 to forty-six per cent in 1973. The percentage in the *Nova* sample was thirty-six per cent.

We can then, excluding advertising and illustrations (but remembering their predominant and often linked effect), look at the distribution of remaining editorial material between different kinds of interest. Table 16(a) shows the 1961 distribution.

Table 16(a)

July 1961	Editorial comment	House and cooking	Shopping guide	Personal appearance	Advice on behaviour	Letters	Fiction	Gossip	Medical	Arts	Travel	Children	Animals	Careers
Woman's Own	10	11	1	14	6	3	38	12	2	3	—	—	—	—
Woman's Mir.	10	5	6	11	—	4	15	36	7	1	—	5	—	—
She	17	6	17	3	3	4	6	13	1	8	14	2	6	—
Vogue	5	6	49	10	—	—	—	7	—	19	4	—	—	—
*Honey**	10	—	1	21	7	4	26	11	2	6	8	—	—	4
*Boyfriend**	5	—	—	8	13	—	47	25	—	2	—	—	—	—

The variations here are interesting, from the preponderance of fiction and gossip in the cheaper magazines to the emphasis on consuming ('buying advice') in the more expensive (the sections on arts and travel in the latter are in some ways simply 'buying advice', in line with a whole tendency in extended 'consumer' interests and habits). More important, however, than these variations of type was the general exclusion, in the 1961 sample, of almost all reference to public affairs. This was then a deliberately limited 'woman's world'. However the 'non-political' world which this exclusion created was not without its clear and insistent social values, of consumption, personal competition and (as may be seen in the later analysis of fiction from this sample) 'social success'.

A comparable analysis was made in 1965, and is shown in Table 16(b).

Table 16(b)

July 1965	Editorial material	House and cooking	Shopping guide	Personal appearance	Advice	Letters	Fiction	Gossip	Medical	Arts	Travel	Children	Animals	Careers
Woman's Own	—	12½	1½	15	13½	5	29	3	3	1	—	7½	9	—
Woman's Mirror	12	10½	1	7	2½	7	24	23	2	—		9	2	—	—
She	4	9	8½	5	8½	3	10	8	4	12	5	7	1	15
Vogue	5	23	13	8	6	—	—	—	—	25	20	—	—	—
*Honey**	14½	—	7	12	14½	2	34	6½	—	2½	—	—	—	7
*Boyfriend**	6	—	3½	10	5½	2	60†	8	—	5	—	—	—	—

† 83 per cent of this fiction is in strip cartoon form.

By comparison with the earlier sample, it is clear that the interests represented in women's magazines have been significantly broadening. It is not only that, in the 1965 sample, there were occasional articles of general public interest, but that a magazine like *She*, for example, within its woman's magazine make-up, was in some ways comparable to older kinds of general interest picture magazines. In the same direction, advice on behaviour, which had been normally confined to discussion of problems of emotional relationship, added to this still substantial emphasis a new kind of advice on legal and financial problems (one feature, for example, was called 'Finance for Females').

In another sense, of course, certain of the magazines consist almost entirely of advice on behaviour, through a very wide range of approaches and techniques. Significantly, it is often difficult to separate such advice on behaviour from the most detailed kind of shopping guide. A special comment is necessary on such magazines as *Vogue* and *Honey*. In *Vogue*, of course, every other interest is subordinated to the display of clothes, but what is most remarkable is an extraordinary integration of other interests into this emphasis. Travel interest, for example, is absorbed into the photographs of clothes, with an emphasis that the background is 'real desert' (place indicated). Being in that place and having those clothes (shopnames and prices overprinted) are decisively brought together. But buying the clothes is an entry to more than this: a *Vogue* feature on picnics, for example, began with three to four hundred words of an article on picnics in history and art, continued at the back of the magazine where it ran among the advertisements, but continued also in another form in seventeen and a half pages of pictures; reproduction of part of Tissot's painting, *The Picnic*, and then staged photographs putatively illustrating famous picnics in literature, from Dryden's *All for Love* – Cleopatra on the Nile, 'shimmering seductive silk tunic, Eastern blue fringed with golden lace, flowering pearly gold and silver roses; 55 gns. . . .

Nile picnic prepared by the New Winter Palace Hotel, Luxor' – to Oscar Wilde – a group in the woods, with precise shopping details not only of the clothes but of the birdcage which happens to be hanging in one of the trees. The reader was offered the art, the quotations, the little article, the clothes, the accessories, the photographs, the authors' names and the travel in a single operation. *Honey* had a further variation of this: an abridged story, called 'A Dream of a Holiday', which ran through seventeen pages, mainly of pictures illustrating episodes in the story ('a package holiday with . . . I hoped, a package romance thrown in'), in which the clothes worn by the characters were on the same page given shop and price details. The reorganization of wide areas of interest around advertising and a shopping guide has now gone very far indeed. At the same time, a way of life and values belonging to this same integration have been tirelessly projected. In the 1965 *Honey*, for example, most of the advice was on careers, which were mainly interpreted as careers as secretaries, and often as secretaries in just this world: 'the jobs in which a bright girl stands a good chance of getting ahead are usually in Advertising, Public Relations, magazines, newspapers, t.v. and publishing'; note, in publishing 'secretaries can progress fairly rapidly to assistants and readers'. There were picture guides and written advice on how to behave at an interview, how to prepare for travel as a secretary, and how to acquire knowledge in ways useful in this world: for example, a secretary should be in a position to say to her boss, 'the monsoons tend to make it rather damp in Delhi in August, so don't forget your raincoat'. The impression left was of a magazine teaching partly educated people not just what to consume and how, but which trends in the society to condition themselves to. And at this point we are analysing not so much a *distribution* of interests as their *integration*: basically around advertising, and with a superstructure of the projected values of a public relations world. The older type of woman's magazine can be interestingly compared with these versions of a broadening of horizons.

A further comparative analysis was made in 1973, and is shown in Table 16(c).

Table 16(c)

July 1973	Opinion	Editorial	House & Cookery	Shopping Guide	Personal appearance	Advice	Letters	Fiction	Gossip	Medical	Arts	Travel	Children	Animals	Careers	Finance
Woman's Own	3	8	23	6½	6	6½	3	25	13	6	—	—	—	—	—	—
Vogue	—	6	6	15	12	—	—	—	25	6	10	6	—	—	—	4
Honey*	3	11	—	16	17	3	1½	23	9	7½	3	6	—	—	—	—
Nova	23	7	8	3	5	—	2	7	12	7	11	6	—	2	—	7

This analysis shows some further significant changes. Most striking is that represented by the new category of 'opinion', articles beyond the range of what had been considered 'women's interests' in 1961, on such matters as capital punishment, equal pay, cost of living, the women's liberation movement. There are also more general interest items, some of them expressed in local 'magazine' format, with small pieces on politics, the arts and personalities side by side. In the category of house and cooking there is a change of content from housekeeping in the older sense, in cooking especially, where there is an emphasis on where to buy exotic foods and where to eat out. The shopping guides – 'buying advice' – remain quite similar; there are still full-page fashion illustrations using live models, overprinted with details of cost and where to buy. These still have linking 'editorial' themes, as in one example of clothes related to the (Hollywood) Wild West. Advice on personal behaviour is somewhat reduced, as is fiction, and medical advice has increased, and now includes psychological perspectives on health. At the same time items about children have been markedly reduced and in some cases excluded. A new specialized category is advice about financial matters, normally investment, of the kind seen in the case of newspapers as markedly increasing during the sixties. Pieces about careers have been reduced or have disappeared, in their older forms, and have been replaced by what is in effect a folding-in of careers to almost all other interests. In general the magazines are both less limited and less 'homely'. They are addressed to women of wider interests, and also to a characteristic model of the employed 'socialized' woman.

We have been looking so far at printed material, in newspapers and magazines. We can now look at broadcast material, which is probably even more important. Tables 17(a) and (b) show the distribution of interests in a sample week's television programmes in 1961 and 1965. The tables show hours and minutes.

Table 17(a)

July 1961	News	Documentaries	Discussions	Music (general)	Music (popular)	Panel games	Variety	Religious	Hobbies	Sport	Advertising magazine
B.B.C.	4·40	6·20	2·10	3·00	1·40	0·30	3·40	1·53	0·35	7·50	—
I.T.V.	3·13	2·30	2·20	—	2·05	3·20	3·50	2·30	0·45	2·45	0·45

Both in 1961 and in 1965 there were less significant differences between B.B.C. and I.T.V. than between different sectors of the press. The simpler models of 'serious' and 'popular' interest, which had become stabilized in differing types of newspaper, were in effect bypassed in television. and

Table 17(b)

July 1965	News	Documentary	Music (general)	Music (popular)	Education	Panel games	Variety	Religion	Children	Hobbies	Sport
B.B.C. 1	3·00	8·55	0·50	1·20	0·35	0·25	4·30	2·05	4·30	—	14·00
I.T.V.	3·08	7·30	—	1·10	0·45	0·30	4·45	3·00	5·15	1·10	6·25
B.B.C. 2	2·59	5·30	1·35	0·55	1·45	—	1·35	0·30	2·05	0·50	7·2

in this perspective can be seen as residual. There have been, of course, important differences of emphasis in programming, and these can be seen again in a more extended comparative analysis, from 1973, in which we can look at the distribution of interests not only in the three British television programmes but also in two contrasting United States television services: a public channel, K.Q.E.D. (San Francisco) and a commercial channel, Channel 7 (California). The comparison has a special relevance because of the great

Table 18. Programme Distribution by Hours

Sample week: March 1973	B.B.C. 1	B.B.C. 2	Anglia	K.Q.E.D.	Ch. 7
A. *News and Public Affairs*					
News	5·7	3·5	5·0	5·2	11·6
News mag. (gen.)	7·1	—	5·1	5·1	5·3
News mag. (ethnic)	3·1	—	—	2·5	0·3
Public affairs dis.	8·3	4·3	3·0	8·5	1·8
	24·2	7·8	13·1	21·3	19·0
B. *Features and Documentaries*					
Features	5·6	6·2	4·5	4·5	0·6
Documentaries	1·0	5·9	2·0	1·0	—
	6·6	12·1	6·5	5·5	0·6

Table 18. Programme Distribution by Hours — continued

Sample week: March 1973	B.B.C. 1	B.B.C. 2	Anglia	K.Q.E.D.	Ch. 7
C. Education					
Schools, colleges, etc.	17·9	16·5	10·7	18·6	—
Instructional	2·9	1·7	2·2	3·5	0·9
Adult education	1·9	—	—	2·5	2·0
	22·7	18·2	12·9	24·6	2·9
D. Arts and Music	1·2	1·7	—	4·5	—
E. Children's Programmes					
Cartoons, puppets	4·4	0·1	1·1	—	2·5
Other entertainment	1·4	0·7	4·6	—	2·0
Educational	5·7	3·3	2·6	25·0	0·8
	11·5	4·1	8·3	25·0	5·3
F. Drama					
Plays	4·4	3·1	3·5	—	—
Series	6·3	0·9	8·7	1·0	16·3
Serials	0·8	1·5	8·1	3·7	6·1
	11·5	5·5	20·3	4·7	22·4
G. Movies	6·7	6·6	12·3	5·2	23·8
H. General Entertainment					
Musical shows	2·7	3·0	2·0	—	1·1
Variety shows	1·2	0·5	3·7	—	0·4
Games, quiz shows	1·5	1·0	3·2	—	15·9
Talk shows	2·0	—	0·9	—	15·0
	7·4	4·5	9·8	—	32·4
I. Sport	5·9	1·1	6·7	2·0	6·4
J. Religion	1·1	—	0·6	—	0·8
K. Publicity (internal)	1·1	0·7	1·7	1·4	1·4
L. Commercials	—	—	10·8	—	18·4
Total Hours	99·9	62·3	103·0	94·2	144·3

influence of American programming on British television,
but some significant differences emerge from it, and perhaps
especially the lesser degree of polarization between 'public-
service' and 'commercial' types of television in Britain,
where the basic orientation to 'public service', though
constantly under attack, still effectively survives.

Since total hours in these five services vary so considerably,
it will be helpful to see the distribution of interests expressed
in percentages of total material broadcast. These are shown
in Table 19.

*Table 19. Comparative Percentages in Programme Category
Distribution*

Sample week: March 1973	B.B.C. 1	B.B.C. 2	Anglia	K.Q.E.D.	Ch. 7
News and Public Affairs	24·5	12·0	13·0	22·5	14·0
Features and Documentaries	6·5	20·0	6·3	6·0	0·5
Education	23·0	29·5	12·5	26·0	2·0
Arts and Music	1·0	2·5	—	5·0	—
Children's Programmes	11·5	6·5	8·0	27·0	4·0
Drama – plays	4·5	4·5	3·1	—	—
Drama – series and serials	7·0	4·0	16·6	5·0	17·0
Movies	6·5	11·0	12·0	5·5	18·0
General Entertainment	7·5	7·5	9·5	—	24·5
Sport	8·0	1·5	6·2	2·0	4·5
Religion	1·0	—	0·6	—	0·5
Publicity	1·0	1·0	1·5	1·0	1·0
Commercials	—	—	10·7	—	14·0

We can then distinguish, in very general terms, two types of
programming, 'public service' and 'commercial', and see
how these compare, both between different channels and,
in the case of the British channels, over a period. 'Public
service' programming (Type A) includes news, public
affairs, features, documentaries, education, arts, music, plays,
sport, and programmes for children. 'Commercial' pro-

gramming (Type B) includes drama series and serials, movies and general entertainment (including variety and panel games). The comparisons are shown in Table 20.

Table 20.
Comparative Percentages of Types of Programming

	Type A	Type B
July 1961		
B.B.C.	70	30
I.T.V. (Anglia)	49	51
July 1965		
B.B.C. 1	63	37
B.B.C. 2	67	33
I.T.V. (Anglia)	51	49
March 1973		
B.B.C. 1	78·5	21·5
B.B.C. 2	78	22
I.T.V. (Anglia)	57	43
K.Q.E.D. (U.S.A.)	89	11
Channel 7 (U.S.A.)	31	69

Note: commercial advertising is omitted throughout; its relative percentages, in applicable cases, are shown in Table 19.

This shows the continuing general difference between B.B.C. and I.T.V. types of programming, after a period in which they had seemed to be moving together. The British commercial channel is very much nearer the 'public service' type than the American commercial channel; this is an effect of different political structures in broadcasting, and of the competitive effect (which works also the other way, affecting B.B.C. programming) of relatively equal types of service. The American comparison is more extreme, and it should be said that there are strong pressures to adapt

British television to its model, of a majority 'commercial' service and a minority 'public' service, with the probable effects on programming that can be observed.

There are more emphatic differences in the distribution of interests in the various B.B.C. sound radio programmes. Table 21 sets out a sample week's distribution.

It used to be said that the B.B.C. sound programmes formed a pyramid of separate levels of taste and interest and seriousness, on which listeners might move from the base of the Light through the middle level of the Home to the apex of the

Table 21(a)

July 1961	Home	Light	Third	Network Three
	h.m.	h.m.	h.m.	h.m.
News	15·50	6·25	—	—
Magazine	10·35	6·30	—	—
Documentary	4·50	2·10	1·00	—
Discussion	7·30	1·00	2·40	1·30
General Talks	5·35	0·30	3·30	0·50
General Readings	2·40	1·50	—	—
Poetry	—	—	1·35	—
Music (general)	30·20	7·25	9·50	1·00
Music (popular)	7·30	71·20	—	—
Opera	1·30	—	4·50	—
Drama (classic)	—	—	0·35	—
Drama (general modern)	2·30	1·30	1·30	—
Drama (serials)	—	4·45	—	—
Drama (adventure)	3·05	0·30	—	—
Drama (crime)	2·00	1·00	—	—
Children	2·10	1·55	—	—
Hobbies	0·30	—	—	1·15
Languages	—	—	—	—
Sport	2·50	6·10	—	—
Variety	2·30	9·30	—	—
Panel games	2·00	1·00	—	—

Table 21(b)

July 1965	Home	Light	Third	Network Three
	h.m.	h.m.	h.m.	h.m.
News	18·30	4·00	1·10	1·32
Religion	6·45	0·25	0·20	—
Magazine	26·35	—	—	—
Documentary	3·15	—	2·00	—
Discussion	3·15	1·30	2·25	—
General Talks	4·03	—	2·40	—
General Readings	4·00	1·15	—	—
Poetry	—	—	1·35	—
Music (general)	13·00	—	13·10	52·30
Music (popular)	9·05	114·40	—	1·30
Opera	—	—	1·55	0·30
Drama (classic)	—	—	1·00	—
Drama (general modern)	6·45	2·10	2·10	—
Drama (serials)	4·45	4·00	—	—
Drama (adventure)	0·30	1·00	—	—
Drama (crime)	0·30	—	—	—
Children	3·35	—	—	—
Education (+languages)	1·30	—	—	5·00
Hobbies	2·30	—	—	—
Sport	1·48	1·50	—	19·15
Variety	1·30	5·30	—	—
Panel Games	3·40	1·10	—	—

Third. This is not now B.B.C. policy, which has been defined as the provision of planned alternative listening. Obviously general policy has been affected by the coming of television as a majority service, but quite apart from that there was a characteristic movement, through the period, towards cultural specialization. The specialized distribution in music programmes shows this especially clearly. Similarly the complex of news, magazine, documentary and discussion programmes, represented in 1961 by a ratio of 3·5 Home to 1 Light, was in 1965 a ratio of 9 to 1, and in 1973, after the

Table 21(c)

July 1973	Radio 4	Radio 1	Radio 2	Radio 3
	h.m.	h.m.	h.m.	h.m.
News	17·20	0·39	2·17	2·50
Religion	3·58	0·18	1·13	0·20
Magazine	32·28	3·07	6·07	1·40
Documentary	4·35	0·55	—	—
Discussion	7·30	—	—	5·55
General Talks	4·50	0·20	0·28	1·35
General Readings	5·40	—	—	1·35
Poetry	0·35	—	—	0·45
Music (general)	7·12	5·36	12·32	71·25
Music (popular)	—	98·33	39·01	0·25
Opera	—	—	—	5·55
Drama (classic)	3·30	—	—	1·30
Drama (general modern)	8·50	—	—	0·20
Drama (serials)	4·30	—	4·30	—
Drama (adventure)	0·45	—	—	—
Drama (crime)	—	—	—	—
Children	2·15	—	0·07	—
Education and Language	0·30	—	—	5·00
Education (v.h.f. only)	10·00	—	—	—
Hobbies	1·45	—	—	—
Sport	1·00	1·12	24·34	14·05
Variety	0·30	0·29	8·25	—
Panel Games	4·52	2·28	0·28	—
Farming	2·10	—	—	—

further specialization of services into Radios One to Four, was 16 Radio Four to 1 Radio One and 6 Radio Four to 1 Radio Two. It remains to be seen whether these tendencies, which were significantly affected by competition from 'pirate' and commercial stations, will be in any way reproduced with the development of more television (including cable) channels. For in some ways, even under the same public authority, television is now unique, in British communications, in attempting to combine diverse interests into

a general service. This is evidently a matter of basic communications policy.

ANALYSIS

From measurement by categories we can see something of the
distribution of interests in various kinds of paper and programme. Yet to see the full body of what is communicated we
have to look at the varying ways in which these interests are
presented.

Headlines

We can learn a good deal about the tone and interest of particular newspapers simply by comparing headlines. Here is
a sample of main headlines from an average week in 1961:

MONDAY

Times	RUSSIA DISPLAYS HER AIR POWER
Guardian	RUSSIA SHOWS OFF HER AIR POWER
Telegraph	RUSSIA DISPLAYS HER MISSILES
Mail	MR K'S SKY-OPENER
Express	KRUSCHEV SHOWS OFF
Herald	THE MIGHTIEST OF ALL AIR SHOWS — BY MR K
Worker	PRICE-RISE, PAY-PEG PLAN
Mirror	CRUTCHES FOR THE DUKE
Sketch	ROPED CHILD FOUND IN LAKE

TUESDAY

Times	MR KENNEDY ORDERS DEFENCE REVIEW
Guardian	MR KENNEDY ORDERS DEFENCE REVIEW
Telegraph	MENZIES CLASH ON COMMON MARKET
Mail	SIX SAY: LET'S TALK
Express	SANDYS C AND B MENZIES O
Herald	THE SIX CALL BRITAIN TO TALKS ON AUGUST I
Worker	WELCOME SPACEMAN!

| Mirror | STUFFED SHIRTS IN THE SPACE AGE |
| Sketch | RAF BOFFIN WILL QUIZ GAGA |

WEDNESDAY

Times	CHEERING CROWDS HAIL MAJOR GAGARIN
Guardian	HERO'S WELCOME FOR MAJOR GAGARIN
Telegraph	GAGARIN LUNCH WITH QUEEN
Mail	SHAKE! 2,000 TIMES
Express	FANTASTICHEVSKY
Herald	LONDON GIVES LITTLE YURI THE BIG HAND
Worker	A REAL HERO'S WELCOME
Mirror	RADY VAS VIDJETJI
Sketch	GA-GA OVER GAGA

THURSDAY

Times	US MISSILE DETECTOR LAUNCHED
Guardian	MISSILE TRACKER IN ORBIT
Telegraph	COMMANDOS WILL QUIT KUWAIT
Mail	PREMIER TO WARN
Express	RED EXPERTS PERISH
Herald	US PUTS 'SPY IN THE SKY' OVER RUSSIA
Worker	PANZERS HERE IN AUTUMN
Mirror	THE GIRL WHO GAVE YURI A KISS
Sketch	1-TON WHALE AMOK AT KEW

FRIDAY

Times	EMERGENCY ACTION TO RESTORE ECONOMY
Guardian	SHIPYARDS INQUIRY BY GOVERNMENT
Telegraph	PREMIER ANXIOUS BUT 'NO FEARS'
Mail	MAC PLAYS IT CALM
Express	WORRIED — NOT AFRAID
Herald	I'M WORRIED BUT NOT AFRAID, SAYS PREMIER
Worker	BAN-BOMB: SMASHING VICTORY
Mirror	BURIED ALIVE!
Sketch	THIS IS MY AXE

SATURDAY

Times	GEN. KASSEM RENEWS CLAIM TO KUWAIT
Guardian	FBI MISGIVINGS ON COMMON MARKET
Telegraph	TUC TO MEET ON ETU CRISIS
Mail	STRIKE HALTS BOAC
Express	STRIKE STOPS PLANES
Herald	THE CRISIS: TORIES NOW TURN TO PLANNING
Worker	MAC PLANS A WAGE CUT IN DISGUISE
Mirror	TUC PROBE SHOCK FOR RED UNION
Sketch	BOAC STRUCK DEAD

These may be compared with further examples. Here is a sample of Sunday newspaper headlines (July 1965):

SUNDAY

Times	US WANTS TO SEAL OFF N VIETNAM AND EXTEND BOMBING
Observer	CALLAGHAN PUTTING US IN PAWN — LLOYD
Telegraph	HEATH DAMAGED BY COUP THAT COLLAPSED — CLUMSY INTRIGUE
Express	NEW RAIL THREAT AS GO-SLOW SPREADS
People	LOUSIEST SUMMER IN YEARS
News of the World	WHY I ESCAPED — BY BIGGS
Citizen	WILSON SLAMS WORK-TO-RULE
Mirror	IT'S HEARTBREAK AT THE FORUM

We have become used to this familiar range of emphasis within the British Press. It is worth comparing the newspaper headlines of two sample days with the headlines of the B.B.C. morning news bulletins:

MONDAY, 5 JULY 1965

B.B.C.	Extra police were sent to the American Embassy in London last night after a home-made bomb had exploded at the West End Office of the American Express Company.

At least twelve people were killed and hundreds injured when a whirlwind swept across Northern Italy.

American bombers, based on Guam Island, have again attacked Vietcong guerillas in South Vietnam.

The Transport and General Workers conference begins today. The Acting General-Secretary says he thinks delegates will reject the Government's Incomes Policy.

A cloudy day, with sunny intervals, is forecast for all districts.

Times	US BANS ATTACKS ON MISSILE SITES
Guardian	MR GRIMOND WARNS OF DANGER TO WEST
Telegraph	BOMB AT LONDON US AGENCY
Mail	INSIDE SOUTH AFRICA'S GAOLS
Express	BOMB BLAST DRAMA
Sun	MR EXPORTS SHOWS HOW
Worker	BELT UP — STICK TO POLO
Mirror	PEER JOINS ROW OVER THE DUKE
Sketch	MP'S CLASH OVER PHILIP

SATURDAY, 10 JULY 1965

B.B.C.   A man in West London has given the police information about the furniture van used in the Wandsworth Jail break.

In Washington, the House of Representatives has passed the Bill to give Negroes the vote unconditionally.

General Franco's new Cabinet has promised a more representative political set-up for Spain.

Queen Anne-Marie of Greece has given birth to a daughter.

North Vietnam has ruled out any question of meeting the Commonwealth peace mission.

Some Labour backbench M.P.s are campaigning this week-end over the issue of Parliamentary privilege.

A mainly dry day is forecast, although there's a
chance of rain spreading into western areas later.

Times	HANOI REJECTION OF BRITISH OVERTURE
Guardian	LBJ FORECASTS WORSENING OF VIETNAM WAR
Telegraph	COUNTRY HOUSE HUNT FOR BIGGS
Mail	I PAINTED THE ESCAPE VAN
Express	SHOTGUN DRAGNET
Sun	BIGGS TEAR-GAS SIEGE
Worker	JOHNSON'S VIETNAM THREAT
Mirror	150 POLICE RAID MANSION – BUT NO BIGGS
Sketch	CLUE OF THE RED VAN – MAN TALKS TO YARD

The selection of its main story, by each newspaper, can be
compared with the selection of items by the B.B.C. The order
of priority within the B.B.C. bulletins also deserves scrutiny.
(Note: it should be remembered that there is some difference
in times of news becoming available, between the papers and
the broadcast bulletins. The main differences, however, seem
little related to this fact, in these examples.)

One further kind of comparison can be made, between
headlines indicating main news stories in British and other
newspapers on a particular day. The following examples come
from 7 and 8 December 1965 in the British morning papers and
in a random selection of newspapers in other countries:

7.12.65

Le Monde (Paris)	GENERAL DE GAULLE IS EXPECTED TO DECIDE BEFORE THURSDAY EVENING TO MAINTAIN HIS CANDIDATURE IN THE SECOND BALLOT
New York Times	DE GAULLE SILENT ON RUNOFF ROLE; ENTRY EXPECTED
La Stampa (Turin)	DE GAULLE WILL PRESENT HIMSELF TO THE BALLOT WITH MITTERRAND
Berlingske Tidende (Copenhagen)	THE GENERAL IS SILENT, BUT MUST SHOW UP BY THURSDAY AT LATEST

Izvestia (Moscow)	THE JUST CAUSE OF VIETNAM WILL TRIUMPH
Frankfurter Allgemeine	AFTER THE FAILURE IN THE ELECTION: DE GAULLE IS SILENT
Expressen (Stockholm)	GHOST PLANE WITH DEAD PILOT OVER SWEDEN
Times	GENERAL DE GAULLE READY FOR SECOND BALLOT
Guardian	LBJ SUMMONS CHAIRMAN OF RESERVE BANK
Telegraph	JOHNSON SENDS FOR BANK CHIEF
Mail	LUNIK BUMP-DOWN
Express	'STOP THIS DEAL'
Sun	BROWN FACES CABINET CRITICS
Worker	CALL TO BEAT DE GAULLE
Mirror	BOOKIES BAN HUGE PAY-OUT ON DOGS COUP
Sketch	DOGS COUP BOOKIES WON'T PAY OUT YET

8.12.65

Figaro (Paris)	DE GAULLE CANDIDATE IN SECOND BALLOT
New York Herald-Tribune	VATICAN COUNCIL ENDS: BIRTH CONTROL IN DOUBT
Die Welt	ROME COUNCIL ENDS TODAY
Pravda (Moscow)	ON THE STATE PLAN FOR THE DEVELOPMENT OF THE NATIONAL ECONOMY OF THE USSR FOR 1966
People's Daily (Peking)*	ON THE 20TH ANNIVERSARY OF THE PEOPLE'S RADIO, CHAIRMAN MAO, CHAIRMAN LIU AND OTHER LEADING COMRADES IN THE PARTY AND COUNTRY URGE MAKING GOOD BROADCASTS TO SERVE THE PEOPLE OF CHINA AND THE WHOLE WORLD

* Issue of 9th December, as nearest available.

Times	TWO GOVERNMENT VOICES ON MR SMITH
Guardian	MR BOTTOMLEY CALLS MR SMITH A LIAR
Telegraph	SMITH LIED, SAYS BOTTOMLEY
Mail	CHRISTMAS-EVE BUS THREAT
Express	MOORS: 'DEATH BOASTS' DRAMA
Sun	STOP OIL SHIP, DEMAND MP'S
Worker	'STOP OIL FOR SMITH'
Mirror	MOOR COURT TOLD OF MURDER BY AXE
Sketch	COUPLE JOKED AFTER MURDER WITH AXE

Presenting a story

The briefest comparison of headlines shows obvious variations in the story considered most important, in its presenttation or angling, and in language and tone. It is worth following these aspects through the presentation of one story, from the same week's papers.

The story chosen was the debate and vote on foreign policy and defence at the 1961 conference of the Transport and General Workers' Union. There had been considerable advance commentary and speculation on the result of this debate, but the actual result was given first place in the day's news by only one paper, the *Worker*, which alone has an editorial policy close to the policy supported by the conference. It is fair to assume that if the vote had gone the other way, this situation would have been reversed.

The Times gave the report 23 c.i. (column inches) on a subsidiary news page; the *Guardian* 22 c.i. in the lower middle of the front page; the *Telegraph* $11\frac{7}{8}$ c.i. on front and back pages, and $34\frac{1}{2}$ c.i. on a back inside page; the *Mail* 23 c.i. on an inside page; the *Express* 28 c.i. on the front page; the *Herald* $\frac{3}{4}$ c.i. on the front page and $62\frac{1}{4}$ c.i. on a back inside page; the *Worker* 30 c.i. in a front page lead story; the *Mirror*

$23\frac{1}{4}$ c.i. on an inside page; the *Sketch* $13\frac{1}{4}$ c.i. on an inside page.

In all headlines, except those of the B.B.C. Home Service News and the *Worker*, the issue was personalized in Mr Cousins, the General Secretary. The B.B.C. headline was: 'The Transport Union has reaffirmed its Ban the Bomb policy by a 4 to 1 vote'. The *Worker* headline was: 'Ban-Bomb: Smashing Victory'. Other headlines were: *The Times*: 'Mr Cousins Wins Fight to keep Unilateralism'; *Guardian*: 'Mr Cousins holds Transport Union to Unilateralism'; *Telegraph*: 'Mr Cousins's majority shrinks'; *Mail*: 'Cousins triumphs over Bomb Vote'; *Express*: 'The Winner – Battling Cousins'; *Herald*: 'Cousins Wins by 3 to 1' and on its front page 'The Odd-One-Out'; *Mirror*: 'H-Bomb Victory for Cousins'; *Sketch*: 'Cousins Wins Bomb Battle'.

On this issue, there can be legitimate differences of political interpretation, but reduction to this extreme kind of personalization is in fact a familiar method of angling news. The use of phrases like 'bomb battle' and 'battling Cousins', and in subsidiary headlines 'bomb bout', 'rebel line', 'bomb vote', is also in effect prejudicial. The same is true of the *Worker*'s 'smashing victory'. In the *Express* this effect is underlined by a cartoon showing Mr Cousins as a boxer, with his foot on the chest of Mr Gaitskell. A different effect is achieved by the *Herald*'s use of 'the odd-one-out'. All these devices are familiar ways of inserting a political or emotional interpretation of the news into its actual reporting. A response to the news is powerfully suggested, either before the news is given or in the course of giving it.

The point about personalization has to be assessed from the actual report of speakers in the debate. *The Times* report gives fifty-two speakers for the successful motion, and thirty-five for an alternative motion, with one 'undecided'. These figures are repeated in the *Guardian, Telegraph, Herald, Mail,*

Mirror; the *Express* gives fifty-two and thirty-five. The *Worker* gives no figures, and no breakdown. The *Sketch* gives 'more than eighty', and the B.B.C. gave 'nearly a hundred'. In all reports but that in *The Times*, the groups of speakers are interpreted: as 'unilateralists' and 'multilateralists' in the *Guardian*; as 'unilateralists' and 'Gaitskell supporters' in the *Telegraph*; as 'for unilateralism' and 'for collective dis-armament' in the *Mail*; as 'for Cousins' and 'for multilateral disarmament' in the *Express*; as 'for Cousins' and 'against' in the *Herald*; as 'for' and 'against' in the *Mirror*. The *Tele-graph* interpretation has to be set against *The Times* report that Mr Gaitskell 'came in for abuse from both sides'. Only the *Telegraph* reports the actual terms of the successful motion, and although the issue had been widely discussed beforehand it is probable that many readers of the other papers would be to some extent uncertain about the exact policy being debated.

Reports of the length of the debate, where given, varied from 'all day' (B.B.C.) and 'day-long' (*Worker*) to 6 hours (*Mail, Express, Mirror*), $5\frac{1}{2}$ hours (*Herald*), and 5 hours (*Times*). Reports of the majority for the successful motion in-cluded '4 to 1' (B.B.C., quoting its Industrial Correspondent's estimate), '4 to 1' (*Mail*), 'between 3 and 4 to 1' (*Mirror*), 'about 590 to 170' (*Telegraph*), '3 to 1' (*Times, Express, Sketch*). The *Guardian* quoted varying estimates of the show of hands, from '5 or 6 to 1' to 'more like 5 to 2', and gave a 'consensus of opinion among a group of reporters' as '3 to 1', while noting that in the circumstances all estimating was 'hazardous'. The *Herald* said that 'some estimates put today's majority even higher than 3 to 1'. It added that of the 769 delegates there were 'at most' 150 hands against. The *Tele-graph* reported that it 'appeared to most observers' that '170 showed their opposition to the General Secretary', though estimates of the minority varied between 100 and 200. The

Express reported '180 against him'. The *Worker* reported the minority as 'less than a tenth'.

Interpretations of the result ranged from 'tremendous personal triumph' (*Mail*), 'striking personal triumph' (*Mirror*), 'his most significant victory' (*Herald*) to the *Telegraph*'s 'the result can be fairly regarded as an achievement for both sides'. Comparisons with the vote of the previous conference ranged from 'majority severely reduced' (*Guardian*), 'majority shrinks' (*Telegraph*), 'far smaller than at last conference' (*Sketch*), to the *Herald*'s comment that at the last conference the majority was '14 to 1', 'but that was in a different context'.

Reports of the actual speeches varied in emphasis. *The Times* reported the proposer and seconder of the successful motion in 3 c.i. and the proposer and seconder of the unsuccessful motion in 4 c.i. It added $\frac{3}{4}$ c.i. and $1\frac{1}{8}$ c.i. general summary respectively. Mr Cousins's speech was reported in $3\frac{1}{4}$ c.i. This balance, 7 c.i. for fifty-two speakers, $5\frac{1}{8}$ for thirty-five speakers, came through elsewhere as: *Guardian*, $7\frac{1}{8}$ and $1\frac{3}{8}$; *Telegraph*, $15\frac{1}{2}$ and $2\frac{1}{4}$; *Mail*, 3 and $2\frac{1}{2}$; *Express*, $1\frac{5}{8}$ and nil; *Herald*, $7\frac{7}{8}$ and $6\frac{1}{8}$; *Worker*, $11\frac{1}{4}$ and nil; *Mirror* $3\frac{1}{4}$ and nil; *Sketch*, $\frac{1}{2}$ and $2\frac{3}{4}$. The largest item in all these reports was the speech of Mr Cousins, except in the *Sketch*.

In the reporting of speeches *The Times* made little comment. The *Guardian* described Mr Cousins as 'like an avenging angel' and his speech as 'powerful if confusing'. The *Telegraph* described Mr Cousins as 'at his most messianic'. The *Mail* reported that he 'thundered passionately'. The *Express* reported 'his tornado of a speech', described it as 'noteworthy as much for its arrogant self-assurance as for its eloquent sincerity', and introduced its limited direct quotation with 'he roared'. The *Herald* reported a 'dramatic speech'. The *Worker* made no comment. The *Mirror* reported 'one of the most powerful speeches of his career' and described thirty-eight minutes of 'impassioned words'. The *Sketch* reported that Mr Cousins 'spoke passionately – in his shirt sleeves'.

'Sex' in the Sunday papers

It has become commonplace to complain that there is too much 'sex' in certain Sunday papers, but it is necessary to analyse this content further. In general, there is a fairly regular association of sex with crime, and a subsidiary association of sex with professional entertainment, particularly with pictures of actresses and models. These associations would seem to determine what is normally meant, in these papers, by 'sex'. Other kinds of report are rare.

Apart from the photographs of actresses and models, and reports of the reputed affairs of film stars and similar personalities, there seem to be two main categories. The papers concerned are principally the *News of the World*, the *People* and the *Pictorial* (*Mirror*). The first category is the reporting of court cases involving adultery, seduction, rape, homosexuality, indecent exposure, and prostitution. The *News of the World* seems to specialize in this kind of report; other papers take up only certain spectacular cases. The reporting is usually quite straight, though the headlines are angled: 'When Her Husband Had to Whistle'; 'At 2 a.m. After a Dance was Over'; '18 Photos in her Dressing-Table Drawer'. Sometimes a case is written up, by a named reporter: 'A Den of Vice in an Old Country Town'.

A second category derives from fact, or alleged fact, but not as regular reporting. One group in this category is that of 'memoirs' or 'confessions', either of persons involved in prosecution or scandal, or of persons prominent in entertainment. These works are advertised and headlined in such ways as 'My Wicked Life' or 'I Was Tempted and I Fell', and it is sometimes implied that they should be read as a warning.

The same implication of moral warning, or a necessary exposure of unpleasant facts, is usually given to another group in this category: 'investigations' undertaken by the newspaper itself. An example is 'The Amazing Double Life of X.Y.' (name and photograph printed) – 'infant teacher and call-girl', advertised as 'by the *People* investigators'. Two reporters, 'acting on information already gathered', made contact with this woman, without disclosing themselves as reporters, to try to prove her 'activities as a prostitute'. A different kind of independent investigation is the report on some place or habit, as in the same issue of the *People*: '"Love-drug" is killing half a million', a report by an independent writer on prostitution and heroin-addiction in the harbour area of Hong Kong. Of this article the paper says: 'It may shock you. But it must be told.'

Some patterns of fiction in women's magazines

Seventy stories, from twenty-two women's magazines, have been read and analysed. The most striking general feature of most of the stories is that they were evidently written to promote a particular psychological process in the reader. The literary skills used are subordinate to this intention. None has any independent literary intentions or merits.

There is an interesting difference between the normal setting of short stories and of serials: the former are usually set in the home, the latter in some 'exotic' environment (Paris, an Australian sheep farm, Iraq). Of forty stories set in the home, thirty-nine are in middle-class homes; the exception is in one of the very cheap fiction magazines. Where stories are set in a place of work, the typical places are offices, hospitals, airports and ocean liners, the countryside. The whole ordinary range of industrial and shop work is only very occasionally touched.

The social status of the hero is usually a point of interest in the story. Of sixty-nine heroes, only two are described without reference to standing at work. Of the other sixty-seven, two are foreign aristocrats, sixty-four are in 'middle-class' jobs, mainly the professions, and are described as successful in them, while one hero was poor but returns successful from Australia. Almost invariably the social standing of the hero, in these terms, is higher than that of the heroine, and the typical engagement or marriage is 'upwards' in this sense. Marrying 'the boss' is quite regular. The ordinary sign of the hero's success is his car, which is often made a point of emotional interest.

The plots of the stories show certain regular patterns. Twenty-seven of the seventy are a familiar kind of intrigue fiction, often in exotic settings, with crises due to misunderstandings and secrets, and most of the scenes set at balls, weddings, and parties. Three others are in effect anecdotes, humorous or ironic in tone, by male authors. The other forty are concerned with the solution of certain typical emotional difficulties. In these, three methods stand out. Seven stories are in intention therapeutic. A situation such as fear of love, or despair at being jilted or deceived, is taken from the point of view of the heroine. The solution here is always adjustment: a child, an animal, a place overcomes the fear of love; the deceived wife adjusts invariably towards husband, children, and home. The emotional tone of these stories is very similar to that of the practical advice columns, which normally advise adjustment to a difficult situation rather than an attempt to change it.

The other thirty-three stories have solutions in wish-fulfilment (fourteen), or in a kind of magical extraction of the difficulty (nineteen). In the former, the plain, unsuccessful, shy, or jilted girl gets the best (most prosperous) husband in the end. The stories are written from her point of view, and the reader is evidently invited to identify with her. In contrast with these stories, where it all somehow (though for no evident reason) comes right in the end, the 'extraction' stories centre on scenes of critical revelation: the rival is shown up in her true (bad) colours and is overcome, or the jealousy was never really necessary (he had never loved the other anyway, in spite of all appearances to the contrary). The world adjusts to the heroine, not by any action on her part, but by a sudden extraction of the painful element. In the wish-fulfilment stories it just quietly adjusts.

Thus, not only are most women's homes and jobs, and most kinds of men, excluded from these stories, but also any kind of persistent problem and any permanently difficult relationship.

Style in advertising (i)

The basic method of commercial advertising has always been exaggeration, from the seventeenth-century notice of a dentifrice which would not only clean the teeth but fix them and prevent them dropping out, to the contemporary advertisement, in a magazine for Africans, of a preparation that will 'cream your skin lighter'. In the search for superlatives, the limits of sense have long been passed ('whiter than white'), and for a generation the natural reaction to this has been capitalized, in humorous exaggeration ('Guinness – Him Strong'), even while the superlatives continue.

There is still some plain recommendation of products, but the more usual method is to associate the product with some other desirable thing: health, love, respect. This kind of association can be almost infinitely graded: from the strip-cartoon, in an African magazine, recommending a kitchen soap as the way to bring friends home (otherwise the curtains are 'all in holes' and you are ashamed), to the full-colour page, in an English magazine, showing a woman in a mink stole, in a fashionable street filled with long expensive cars, with a chauffeur behind her carrying a long expensive sink. ('So Henry said . . . go out and buy one. So I did . . . Simply acres of draining-board. Such a blissful sink.')

But there is another kind of grading, more subtle in its operation. There is the direct promise of a husband or a better job if a particular product, which can be almost anything, is used, and the reaction against this is again exploited by repeating the claim with humorous exaggeration. Then, there is the indirect promise of the same kind, ranging from a simple side-by-side layout of the product and a desirable situation, to the creation of an atmosphere of dream and dreaminess (often by blurred photography and a use of deep colours).

From one week's newspapers, I have in front of me three pictures of yachting, all of which might have been taken at the same time. Each picture occupies three-quarters of the space of the advertisement, and the name of the product is in each case unobtrusive. It is only by inspection that we find them advertising, respectively, bread, a fruit squash, and a bank. From a magazine in the same week, there is a picture of a cool girl in blue surrounded by six men in black and red, all looking up at her from the darkness. This is 'a fabulous feeling that we call "Colour Confidence"': the product is a make-up, and 'pressmen of the world applaud'.

The common appearance of advertisements of this kind, though only a development from the simpler kind in which a packet of pills was placed alongside a drawing of a doctor or nurse, is now very important. In a sense, the product has become irrelevant: the advertiser is working directly on images and dreams. The concentration of such advertisements creates a whole style of life, centred largely in fantasy, which is in effect a common interest of all advertisers rather than the recommendation of particular products. All ordinary values are temporarily overridden by a kind of bastard art, not clarifying experience but deliberately confusing it.*

It is then no surprise, in a half-page of our most serious newspaper, to find, beside a pleasant picture, these words: 'crust of concrete: push of polyanthus. Polyanthus breaks through . . . naturally', and then 'the week-end is the most natural break of all'. This is a recommendation of television advertising, in those controversial 'natural breaks'. It is completed by the small-type promise: 'at the week-end your commercials penetrate deeply'. We can probably agree that this is what it is all about.

Style in advertising (ii) – 'Natural Breaks'

Like so much else that is artificial, conventional and man-made on television, the natural break for commercials seems to be becoming part of a way of life. People who question it, or television advertising in general, must run the risk of being met with 'Not that again,' or of being told that to persist in such thoughts is to declare oneself a member of the new cultural Establishment. Meanwhile, the Establishment that turns out the commercials is palpably, if sometimes ridiculously and annoyingly, present: it is in this way more real than any possible criticism of it – it has, in a word, become natural.

I was reminded how far this naturalization has gone while watching a film the other night on I.T.V. It started, after a natural break, at a few minutes past seven, and at 7.25, 7.43 and 7.55, when I switched off on some remarks about Britain's best-loved medicated shampoo, this film, itself highly commercial, had experienced natural breaks that even Hollywood had not thought of. (It is some indication of how far things have gone that in the cinema, under the most intense commercial pressures, we could and can watch a film

* For a fuller discussion of this point, see the author's 'The Magic System', in *New Left Review*, July 1960.

straight through, before the adverts come up with the ice-cream.) Given the nature of film editing, at times with several breaks a minute, the possibilities seem endless, though I notice that we are allowed a fairly long first run to get us interested, after which the frequency of the natural phenomena that are called 'breaks' seems miraculously to increase.

It is worth considering how this situation was created. A correspondent has recently sent me an illuminating exchange of letters on this matter with the present Chairman of the I.B.A. When the 1953 White Paper was introduced in Parliament it was said on behalf of the Government that at no time would 'interruption' of the programmes be permitted. A month later it was said that there would be 'no interruptions at all unless they are in what are called "natural breaks"'. That was the loophole through which, as a Member of Parliament observed at the time, a coach and four could be driven; and of course has been. One of the early examples of what a natural break might be was between the acts of a two-act play, 'especially if the first act had lasted for an hour and ten minutes'. A later example was between the scenes in *Hamlet*. (One catches the high-cultural atmosphere in which the business was being done.) As things have turned out, with many endorsements and ratifications including the Act of 1964, the fiction of the natural break has come to mean almost anything that can be made to occur, or, as it were, to stop occurring, at an evening's average of three times an hour. To go on calling them natural breaks is, even for advertisers and their friends, straining human nature too far.

Yet of course, as most of us know, the real problem has to be put the other way round. There are presumably people in Commercial Television who sit watching old films for natural breaks to happen. 'When she goes out and slams the door, Bert. Or when he staggers and there's that cut to the vultures.' Whatever creative possibilities these moments may suggest – deodorants? catmeat? – have never been systematically tried: most authorities don't wait for nature – they make it happen. Producers and their writers and performers are given their time slots – as in all programming, but with the difference that within programmes there will be this predictable alien material. Many people put up with it as they put up with the weather: any powerful social system seems to acquire that natural weight. But it is so far from being the only way it could be done that somebody has to keep insisting that it's natural.

My correspondent complained particularly about commercial breaks in a film of a mountaineering expedition and in a concert from St Paul's. He was told, in effect, that advertisers often sponsor expeditions (though these weren't the advertisements complained about) and, of course, that 'the great mass of our viewers' are not offended by breaks for advertising or by the advertising itself. Perhaps there is evidence for this, but if so, it is significant that the calculations for profitable insertion are so fine. If people accepted, or even, as has been said, positively enjoyed, advertising, there would be no need to interest them in a programme to a point where they intend to go on watching and then contrive a commercial break. It could come up at known times and be watched by positive choice. In the Italian and in other television services dependent on advertising revenue there are separate times set aside, and the separation between programmes and advertising, which was supposed to be a principle of British Commercial Television, is then something more than a fiction. But though as yet resisting general sponsorship, British Commercial Television practice is following the basic American convention, though at a much lower frequency and intensity, as can be observed from watching the number of fades and re-establishing shots in

American imports shown on B.B.C. A whole method has followed from this: the dramatic opening sequence before the credit titles, for instance – an interesting experiment which is now commercial routine.

Meanwhile, sponsored sporting events have become so natural, even on B.B.C., that one has to suppose a high correlation between love of horse-racing, athletics, golf, cricket or similar outdoor pursuits and directorships in beer, cigarette, razor-blade and similar companies. A belated but welcome attempt is now being made to stop a loophole on television advertising of cigarettes, but the general problem is much wider. I was watching cricket on television last week and in the close-ups of batsmen at one end was continually puzzled and distracted by the letters 'pworths' apparently growing out of the caps. I eventually got the whole word in its place on the boundary fence, and realized as I did so that there have been times in watching televised football, as the moves were breaking down, when I have wanted play to move upfield so that the half-word glimpsed behind the action might be completed. I have even had some surprises, as in crosswords. So natural has this placing become, even in socialist stadiums, that is it an effort to visualize the planning, the contracts, the camera-angle calculations that put them there. And it is all on the principle that since we enjoy watching a whole range of programmes and events, something else can be directly or indirectly but always profitably inserted, as if it were a natural accompaniment.

I think it is still worth resisting this whole drift. It is, in any case, necessary to expose its naturalism as contrivance. And what goes, all along the line, for Commercial Television, goes also for the encroachments and contrivances that have put what is in effect advertising into public service broadcasting.

Style in advertising (iii) – '*I.T.V.'s Domestic Romance*'

It can only be prejudice that prevents the general reviewing of those programmes between programmes that are now so important a part of television. Recently, for example, I watched a 35-minute programme (I.T.V.) into which, I do not doubt, as much care and effort and money had been put as into anything else that evening, and yet, to judge by what the reviewers said, it might never have been put out at all. It is true that it was rather intermittent. It ran in short snatches of anything from 45 seconds to about three-and-half minutes, over the period between 5.45 and 10.30 p.m. Nevertheless, it was an interesting blend of naturalism and fantasy, with some clever photography and a few good if recurrent tunes. And it was centred, clearly enough, on domestic issues.

When you think of all the study and research (much of it drawing on the services of professional psychologists and sociologists), of the script conferences, the negotiations on timing, the search through the casting agencies, the rehearsals, the editing, it seems a bit hard that there is no considered reaction at all. Some people say, of course, that the ads aren't art, though they have probably forgotten that every group making them has its creative department, which is even, to prevent misunderstanding, known and referred to as such. Moreover, there is a good deal of mutual voyaging between programmes and commercials. Some of our best directors, it is said, make little programmes about products between their bigger programmes about processes, and many popular performers seem as willing to appear smoking a cigar or eating an ice-cream as doing anything else – murder or detection – that the current script may require. The acting skill needed is in any case approximately the same. Certainly there are plenty of girls who can be guaranteed, after rehearsal, to manage to look coy *and* sultry in the same lingering glance. But try casting a housewife who can repeat 'biological' as if it were a faintly improper suggestion which she's naturally a bit wary of but is by no means certain to refuse. Or the ordinary man, just home from the office, who's depressed thinking he's going to get tinned food for supper and a few minutes later is delighted and affectionate when he gets it out of just the right kind of tin. That, brother (as they say in the trade), is skill.

I want to try then to make amends for this too-long neglect. All this work, all these people, deserve some critical response. It is true I shall have some difficulty in recounting the story-line. It isn't that it wasn't there, but there was this profusion of surface detail: by my account five beers, a cider, four patent drinks, three wines, a tea, three patent medicines, three disinfectants, a flykiller, a hairspray, a toothpaste, five deodorants (though three of these were identical in what seemed the *leitmotif*), bath salts, a bra, high-speed gas, petrol and oil, a razor and two kinds of blade, two newspapers, a paper towel, sweets, two dogfoods and a dog medicine, cigars, tobacco, paint, film, a gardening centre, bread, butter, cheese, a breakfast food, two ice-creams, three kinds of biscuit, salad-dressing, condensed milk, potato mash, chicken pie, tomato ketchup, canned ham and fruit and risotto, two soaps, a washing-powder, and a bottle of washing-up liquid that one of the guest-stars autographed. Describe, describe, as Virginia Woolf said, ironically, about the novels of Arnold Bennett. But then that is where, with this kind of art, we can all very easily go wrong. Perhaps six or seven of these varied things were what you could call described. This feature of the art was indeed almost incidental. What was really there was what happened in the novel after Bennett, when things, objects, became instrumental, active; when it was the life that flowed through and around them that came to count. Take the patent drinks. One, it is true, was being mixed to be drunk. But in the others the flow of feeling was different. A young man and a girl were running by the sea, in the cool spray, and then, in one of those characteristically rapid modern associations of idea, the drink was good, also, for morning sickness. Consider the subtlety of that.

Some people have objected to commercials as the signs of a materialist civilization. Nothing, on this evidence, could be further from the truth. Most of the objects are charms, talismans. A materialist civilization would insist on properties and quantities. The world of this art is different. A girl gets off a plane, and throws up her arm for the photographers. Embarrassment. She goes back, gets the product, comes out again, throws up the other arm. Happiness. But meanwhile our hero (I think it was he) is flying his falcon and drinking his cider (of course, in that order). They meet, after she has run through the woods, and they run together by the sea. When the baby comes they give it a magical cheese which, for boys, could lead to a future as an Olympic athlete, for girls Miss World. They do not forget to wipe its face with a paper towel with a pretty pattern, and they sing while they use it. Nor do they forget to keep theirs a safe home, killing all known germs with a variety of disinfectants. Yet the strains and pressures of living mount. Though she sometimes waltzes round the kitchen, in delight at a new powder, she has trouble keeping him at home until she finds a magic can that opens at both ends, and confesses, another night, when she has bought a prepared chicken pie, that it is making a dishonest woman of her. She keeps using deodorants, hairspray, a toothpaste that gets her noticed and another that gives her confidence, but still she gets pain in those tension areas in the magical map of her head. He, meanwhile, does nothing to stay attractive but shave, though with the most craftsmanlike devices; he is usually, in fact, off on the beer or the cigars. He can sometimes be playful, even imitating a dog to get more tinned food, but though when she is out at the shops she refuses all substitutes (even two for one), he remains hard to please, and she is continually worried that she is not attractive enough or doing enough or that her home isn't safe enough. Still, through the troubles of life, she can always dream. Buy one brand of ice-cream and bearers carry her through the jungle or into a sheik's tent. Buy another and she doesn't even leave home; put on sunglasses, a sunhat and a sunlamp – of course not forgetting the ice-cream – and even though it's raining outside she's on holiday. A last whisk with the flykiller and another anxious, happy, magical day is done.

A story of the way we all try to live now. It makes its effect, really, just because it is intermittent. 'We'll take the break now,' say the I.T.N. news-readers, as if under the weight of the world they need to slip out for a drink. But what the break is really for is this persistent domestic romance: the long suggestive massaging of a skilfully calculated art. What effect does it have? It is impertinent, perhaps, to keep considering effects. Indeed, it comes as a surprise to discover behind this young art – this art of the childhood of the mind and of the second childhood of a kind of society – hard and precise calculations about profit and impact. In a recent paperback* there is an essay by Peter Masson called 'The Effects of Television on Other Media', and the surprise is not only that the central concern is the effect on the advertising media, but that the study is more precise and professional than anything else in the book (things like arts, politics, social behaviour). It seems a long way from that Olympic cheese, but that, perhaps, is how creative art now relates. Behind the scenes, calculation, but in front the pantomime.

*The Effects of Television; ed. Halloran, 1970.

Analysing Television (i)

It is difficult to choose between two kinds of writing about
television. It is possible to isolate particular programmes and
try to analyse them. This is not necessarily what some people
call reviewing: looking at details of performance and
direction. For these can never be isolated from the essential
character of the work, which is not an object to be judged by
its transmission, but a particular structure carrying meanings and values. Yet, in quite another direction, one of the
most obvious elements of television is its quality as sequence.
We can switch on and off for particular programmes but in
some ways the programmes are conceived as a whole and
they're often received as a continuity. I have come to feel
lately that the kind of analysis we most need is of this general
flow: of the organization, the methods and the values within
and through which particular programmes occur.

But these, for many reasons, can be very difficult to see:
above all, because we aren't used to them. For example, one
Friday on B.B.C. 2 I watched a series of programmes from
about eight until past eleven. At various times that evening
there were four solo pieces for which we don't quite have a
name: Peter Cook in a parody of Rod McKuen and his dog,
Alan Bennett in a fairly conclusive parody of Kenneth
Clark's reminiscences of Bernard Berenson, William Rushton
announcing a brave mock-expedition to get away from a
British mood which he described with great accuracy, and
Bernard Braden performing Mark Twain on Fenimore
Cooper. In between these pieces, there were three short films
of India, Georgia Brown singing Brecht, the News and an
episode of *Jude the Obscure*.

The internal effects of this sequence were remarkable.
Cook and Bennett were parodying very recent television programmes which were still clear in the memory, Braden's

cue was the current adaptation of *The Last of the Mohicans*. Rushton's mock-expedition followed an announcement of the B.B.C./*Sunday Times* expedition to Everest and was itself followed by an interview with one of the members of the expedition, who by this time I could hardly listen to because of the prolonged sense of double-take. After Georgia Brown singing the Brecht-Eisler parody of a sentimental ballad, there was a low-keyed discussion of how to prevent expensive paintings leaving Britain while remaining expensive. Capitalist art-dealing was taken for granted and then its marginal consequences worried about. Alan Bennett showed us the conversion of art objects for use in the 'Civilization' game. Next, as a commercial break, the link man showed clips from the week ahead, incidentally playing what was meant to be a sophisticated game with Percy Thrower's gardening programme. Then, following Cook as McKuen, there were two apparent discussions with an American woman on her scheme of physical exercises and with three oddly assorted people on (somewhere, vaguely) Women's Liberation – in which Cook managed to reduce the television interview to the kind of impromptu and sceptical inconsequence on which his own normal performance depends. Then Part Four of *Jude the Obscure* and the edited bits of the News.

What, then, ought really to be said? That this was an ephemeral structure almost instantly parodying itself: a kind of frantic consumption of shadows and responses? But it was not the frequency of parody that was wrong. It was that most of the things being parodied seemed even more insubstantial and artificial than the parodies themselves. Or could one say that the only solid thing there was the attempt on *Jude the Obscure?* But this was television *using* a major English novel with what seemed a quite structural indifference: an object to be adapted and transmitted, the latest classic serial. To pull back and say that Robert Powell was giving a fine performance as Jude, or that the scene at the country wedding (it was actually a town wedding) was pleasant and nicely directed, would be easy but evasive. Deep in this adaptation, the extraordinary and challenging unity of Hardy's theme had been taken apart and put together again in a much smaller action and consciousness. It would be too much to record every minor distortion, every major omission, every gratuitous insertion. Anyone who knows the novel well will have noted them already, and in any case it is the novel that will survive. The real point is the way in which a very difficult and powerful structure of feeling had been made over, as a job, into passable television. The connection with the rest of the evening's events didn't seem too remote. And did it then seem significant that Germaine Greer, in a reduced and disintegrated discussion, could say less about freedom and marriage than even this unrecognizable Sue Bridehead: a voice from 80 years earlier?

Or take the fact that Cook and Rushton in different ways referred to the previous evening's television prize-giving at the Albert Hall. That has certainly provoked some related thoughts, not so much about television as about the paradox I've been trying to get at in its current English usage: this air of mutual congratulation and habitual self-consciousness within a sequence of basically impromptu acts; a brave and busy improvisation through a series of dissolving gestures and images, with just a few steadying shots of the past. Of course I was glad to see Keith Michell's virtuoso performance as Henry VIII applauded. And Eric Morecambe, since his kind of disintegrating scepticism carries the memory of innocence and good will. But it was interesting looking past the synthetic pomp to try to work out the median date of the current show-pieces of English television: *Civilisation*, *The Forsyte Saga*, *The Six Wives of Henry VIII*. It can be done on several projections, some alarmingly far back, but I think the latest and most accurate would centre on Clive Bell, Galsworthy, Korda/Laughton, which I make about 1925. Of course all three are in pictures now. Superb, impressive etc.

The television I find interesting is very different and there was some of it in the same week: *Man Alive* and *World in Action*; the ice-skating and the tennis and the rugby; René Cutforth's helicopter views of Wales; another case for my private dossier on police series in the *Softly Softly* episode on demonstrations; an interesting *Talkback* on the reporting of strikes, and two or three news films.

These programmes tried to deal with events and places that belong to our own world. The *Europa* films of India, though sketchy, belong here rather than in that strange B.B.C. 2 evening. These are programmes within the present real limits of television, and above all, they were not confused by the residual power of other art forms. There was a parallel stage in the evolution of the cinema to what has happened in television. Some of its controllers sought artistic respectability by the transfer of cultural objects that already had prestige: adaptations, famous theatre actors, show places and galleries – and of course the comedians at once parodied them. The real potential of film was meanwhile being developed more directly elsewhere.

I think there is now enough evidence to say that the present controllers of television, after the difficulties of the sixties – difficulties of genuine growth – are turning more and more to the received values of other forms. A work like *Jude* is too resistant for them, it still cuts directly into their own consensus. But the Grand Tour, the Edwardian bourgeoisie, the rollicking and colourful English courtly past: these are static experiences, ready to be upholstered, given the tickets of prestige. A younger generation can do little but mock them, for its own original work is forced out more and more to the edges. The parodists survive, the makers just hang on. But if this is the sequence, I do not see, given everything else that is happening, how it can last much longer.

Analysing Television (ii)

It looked like a dance: the women in white, moving in repeated half-circles, lifting their loose dresses until they swayed like sails. It was a few peasant women in East Africa trying desperately to drive away a huge swarm of locusts which was settling on their crops. If they didn't succeed, or weren't helped, many of their families would starve within the year.

Some help was coming, from a little control room, from a few light planes. And then within a minute we were in another control room, at the top of the Post Office Tower. With a sense of urgency, from this other operations room, we were taken to New York where a chimpanzee was 'giving a press conference'. We had seen the animal before: sponsored by a tea company and with a jacket saying *Daily Mail* on its chest. The press conference was a group of jostling reporters and cameramen shouting 'Hi, Tina,' and similar encouragements. The chimpanzee, so far as I saw, simply moped and mowed. It didn't matter, perhaps. The name of the product got into the camera anyway. I remembered Wordsworth's image, in *The Prelude*, of the blind beggar in the crowded London street, who

> with upright face
> Stood propp'd against a Wall, upon his Chest
> Wearing a written paper, to explain
> The story of the Man, and who he was.
> My mind did at this spectacle turn round
> As with the might of waters, and it seem'd
> To me that in this Label was a type,
> Or emblem . . .

For Wordsworth, 'of the utmost that we know, both of our-

selves and of the universe'. Maybe, but the beggar had put on
his own label. The press conference was another and deeper
kind of alienation. Remembering that field in East Africa,
I recalled Wordsworth's final comment:

> I look'd
> As if admonish'd from another world.

What had produced this conjunction? It was ordinary
B.B.C. 2 planning: a repeat of *The Years of the Locust* followed
by a 'progress report' of the Transatlantic Air Race. The
Horizon film was television at its best: serious, practical,
mobile – a detailed showing of the return of the locust plague,
out of the Arabian desert into a belt across Africa. The people
fighting the locusts had the everyday commitment and com-
radeship of a clear and uncomplicated social purpose. I
remember the Eritrean, a former fighter-pilot, flying his
light plane through the swarm that was bursting on his
windscreen like machine-gun fire: his calm eyes and voice,
his hands on the simple controls. There was a very similar
pilot, an Irishman on Aer Lingus somewhere over the
Atlantic, being interviewed about the Air Race. It took him
several seconds of embarrassed decency to bring out the word
'stunt'. He didn't want to be offensive; he just knew the
difference between that and Alcock and Brown. It isn't often
we get so complete and transparent a festival of the society
so many powerful interests are trying to establish. What was
most remarkable was the combined operation: between the
B.B.C. and the *Daily Mail*; between business firms and the Air
Force and the Navy. This is all critically different from commercial breaks. True, the definition says 'natural breaks'
while in fact most of them are artificial, inside plays and news
programmes. But that is a primitive form. The next stage is
planned integration: a manufactured news event, given a
spurious urgency by reports from a television operations-

room, advertising not only a newspaper and assorted companies but military planes and arms exports. The combined operation is then in turn reported, outside itself, as news.

The transparency is crucial. No insight is needed to see what is happening. When such corporations combine, they don't need to hide. Tuesday's early-evening news bulletin could report, after one crossing, that the makers 'hope to cash in on its unique performance and boost export sales'. The language of a public corporation now comes straight from the popular business columns. And room was found, in a short bulletin on the present condition of the world, for the chimpanzee again, with the comment that as far as the animal was concerned, 'it could have been another T.V. commercial'. And that's it, I suppose: what passes for sophistication: placing it, certainly, but as an accepted and normal event.

They were so short of resources, fighting the locusts. They were poor people in poor countries. It is then not only that the Air Race was a conspicuous waste of resources; in television terms, it was a waste and a diversion of attention. But of course not just to a game. 'A good plane with a lot of commonality', as a Labour Minister recently described a 'multirole combat aircraft'. 'A real winner.' 'Boosting export sales' – to do what? 'Hoping to cash in' – on what? It isn't often that an evening's television dramatizes, so visibly, the conflicts and contradictions of a politically intolerable world.

Europa (B.B.C. 2) made a significant contribution in the same area. It showed a West German film analysing military advertising in various countries. Four million pounds a year in Britain on recruiting commercials: a figure to bear in mind as an index for social service cuts. It was a fine insight into the different ways in which militarism, East and West, sells itself.

After these, after all these, Dürrenmatt's *Conversation a*

Night (*Thirty-Minute Theatre*, B.B.C. 2). This encounter between a freedom writer and his state executioner seemed
curiously abstract. I sensed a disjunction between text and
actors. What freedom could that wraith have written about?
And the philosophical executioner, drawing attention to his
idiosyncrasy, recommending humility as victory? Sad,
empty, resigned: that neutral post-war humanism, with the
knife on stage: sophistication, dwindling down, above empty
streets. Only one line stuck in my mind, connecting to our
own and different world: 'I'm delighted to hear that education is becoming a danger once again.'

SURVEY

Two facts stand out, when we survey the general field of
communications in contemporary Britain. These are, first,
the increasingly close connection between the methods and
content of advertising and editorial material, and, second,
the marked division of material into classes, which then
normally keep to their own world.

The connection with advertising is of several kinds. The
most important is in fact quite difficult to see, unless historical
comparisons are introduced. This is the increasing visual
similarity of newspapers and advertisements, in typography,
layout, and photographic style. Newspapers like *The Times*,
which are still quite traditional in layout,* show this most
clearly by contrast: the regular columns of close print, with
small-type headlines, are very different from the sudden
large headlines, broken-column layout, and the combination
of words and photographs, in a single effect, of the advertisements. The paper's general photographs are separate from
printed news, while its news photographs have usually an

---

* In 1967 this was rapidly changing, to conform in its turn with advertising methods and needs.

immediate relevance to the report. Most advertisement photographs have no direct relevance to the product, or combine some other interest with the product. In the popular newspapers many of the photographs are of this kind, making a direct and often isolated visual appeal. It is difficult, in the popular papers, to separate, at first glance, the news and advertisement photographs, while in layout and typography there is often no distinction between advertising and editorial material. It is then not possible to separate advertising from the general effect of the paper. It is not an isolated item, a kind of support cost, but part of the total communication. The most extreme development of this kind is in the women's magazines, where it is often difficult, without close inspection, to identify an advertisement, and where the verbal and visual styles combine with the similarity of interest to produce a single overall effect. Another relevant case is the advertising supplement, in which apparently independent editorial treatment of products and services is printed alongside direct advertisement, in a planned way.

Historically, the magazine followed the book in style, while the daily newspaper expanded the magazine. The early Sunday newspapers followed printed ballads and broadsheets, with one or two large headlines, and a main illustration, followed by close print. In most newspapers and magazines the style is now that of the advertisement: it was in posters and display advertisements that the use of varied type-sizes, of slogans, and of the planned combination of visual and verbal effect, developed. A neutral look at a two-page spread of a popular newspaper gives the effect of a jig-saw of posters, display advertisments, and display stories. The direction of emotional interest and response by advertising slogans is now directly paralleled in popular newspapers and headlines. In the list of headlines, those from the more traditional papers were consistently easier to understand, as a summary of the main news. Many of the others did not even attempt this, but caught interest, and included emotional reaction, in ways very familiar from general advertising. (Compare the uses of 'axe' and 'dead' in the 1961 *Sketch* headlines, to describe, respectively, economic proposals and grounded aircraft.) Whole pages, planned around headlines of this kind, and around photographs, seem to be aiming to make a single overall emotional effect. Thus a style of communication, developed for the selling of products, has to a considerable extent taken over the presentation of news and opinion.

There is also a connection with advertising in the second general fact: the division of material into classes. Any reasonable survey of the whole content of contemporary communications shows few omissions. Almost any interest and any level of attention is in fact provided for. There are of course striking cases of particular proportions of interest, as in crime and accidents. But most people, choosing from the whole range, could get what they want. Within this general coverage, however, there are quite rigid divisions, and these seem to be increasing.

In magazines and in broadcasting there has been a marked tendency, since the war, to split up general material into particular interests and tastes, rather than covering a general field in a single magazine or service. The old general-interest magazines have mostly gone, to be replaced by special-interest magazines for particular classes of user. The division of broadcasting into Light, Home, and Third programmes, and then, with still further specialization, into Radios One to Four, has had the same fragmenting effect. In television a general programme is still offered, but within this there is a characteristic specialization in relation to hours of viewing: the peak hours, for obvious reasons, carrying programmes of known popular appeal, while new or minority programmes (even for very sizeable minorities) tend to be put into off-peak periods. This is often regrettable, but it is still in many ways better than the division into separate kinds of service which is normal elsewhere.

To many people the development of separate classes of newspaper, magazine and broadcast programme seems natural. In certain cases, of course, the development of specialized media is a sign of cultural growth, which often brings a useful and necessary specialization. This is not, however, in the general field of public communications, the only trend. Two other kinds of pressure are also evident: the pressure of advertisers to have magazines with particular classes of readers who will provide a known market; and the influence of a conventional class-model of British society, divided into upper, middle, and lower groups. The original model of secondary education also assumed three groups, but these are steadily being reduced to two, and there are signs of a similar development in the Press, which now divides much more easily into 'quality' and 'popular', with the steady disappearance of 'middle' papers, than it did a generation ago.

The result is not only that certain interests tend to become specialized to and identified with particular social classes (as, most obviously, serious politics and the traditional arts with the minority). It is also that opportunities for movement between these groups, and for variation of interest within individuals and families, have now to be quite consciously sought. You change your newspaper or magazine, or switch to another service, to make this change of interest. Since individuals and families are in fact very variable, over the whole field, and while classifiable in groups are not as rigidly separate from each other as the differences between newspapers, magazines, and programmes would suggest, this increasing typification is a very serious social tendency. It is worth noting that it is also used, both as a means of social classification ('top people', 'a Third Programme type', 'the average reader of the *Daily Mirror*'), and as a way of recommending papers and magazines, as in general advertising ('discriminating people smoke x; top people read y; go-ahead people drink z'). Meanwhile the evidence of ordinary social and educational investigations reveals no such rigid divisions, but gradual scales of many kinds, which, while reflected in the total content of communications, are not reflected in actual distribution.

There are many genuine problems of communication in a large society which is widely literate yet which has deep educational and social differences. Looking through the material, we see an obvious use of formulas – about a type of reader or listener, and then about his interests and styles and tones. The minority newspapers and magazines can be as rigid in this kind of assumption as the popular productions. Since communication of any kind depends on an element of convention, these formulas can become quite deeply learned, and any growth or change beyond them can be very difficult. We all get used to particular styles and layouts, which have no necessary relevance to the real interests and material, but which we might feel lost without. In actual content and presentation, now, the formulas seem to be hardening: 'the masses' – crime, sex, sports, personalities, entertainment, pictures; 'the minority' – traditional politics, traditional arts, briefings on popular trends. It is then a matter for argument whether 'the masses' and 'the minority' are inevitable social facts, or whether they are communication models which in part create and reinforce the situation they apparently describe.

CHAPTER FOUR

CONTROVERSY

THE MASSES

SURELY we get the culture we deserve. Most things that we produce have to be sold, or they will not go on being produced. Does not this mean, then, that what people are now actually buying is what they want?

Of course [Cecil King, former head of the *Mirror* group, said] you have got to give the public what it wants, otherwise you go out of business as we have seen recently in the case of two or three newspapers. You try and raise its standards as well. The trouble is the critics imagine the great British public is as educated as themselves and their friends, and that we ought to start where they are and raise the standard from there up. In point of fact it is only the people who conduct newspapers and similar organizations who have any idea quite how indifferent, quite how stupid, quite how uninterested in education of any kind the great bulk of the British public are.

Norman Collins, then of Independent Television, added:

If one gave the public exactly what it wanted it would be a perfectly appalling service. . . . It is quite obvious that the educational standard of this country is deplorable. . . . The overwhelming mass of the letters we get are illiterate, they are ungrammatical, they are deplorably written, and what is more distressing, too, they evince an attitude of mind that I do not think can be regarded as very admirable. All they write for are pictures of film stars, television stars, or asking why there are not more jazz programmes, why there cannot be more programmes of a music-hall type. I hold the teachers very largely responsible, if that is the attitude of people in their teens and early twenties. If we provided simply that it would be deplorable.

Now clearly King and Collins had information about public taste. Ought we not simply to accept their conclusions? The masses are stupid and indifferent; we do our best for them, within those limits. The traditional idea of a people wanting light, of democracy as a way of spreading the light, is perhaps merely sentimental. The reality shows otherwise.

But does it, in quite this way? Another kind of evidence comes from research workers and teachers. Joseph Trenaman, Granada Research Fellow, University of Leeds, said:

It is sometimes said that the bulk of the population do not want to learn, they only want to be entertained. This view has no foundation in fact whatsoever. I know of no research or other evidence to support such a view, whereas there is evidence to the contrary. . . . Partly the difficulty is that for less educated people the responses to knowledge are connected with their attitudes to social and class differences, and the plain fact is that what we loosely call culture is identified in their minds with status, with rewards and with power in our society.

Jack Longland, while Director of Education for Derbyshire, said:

Most of these opportunities now for the first time offered by Press and broadcasting, cheap reading, cinema and advertising will continue to be lost if you go on underestimating the intelligence, capacities, tastes and interests of your new mass public. We who are in the business of education have compelling reasons for knowing that this is true. You see, we have met all the members of your future mass-communications society already and have got to know them pretty well.

Longland went on to give examples of the range of creative and voluntary educational activities which most children find excitement and satisfaction in, only to be exposed to 'the full blare of the world of mass communications after school life is over'.

What interests me, in these statements, is the real conflict of evidence. These men were speaking honestly from their experience, in what seems a common field, and reaching quite opposite conclusions. Why?

First, I think, because in fact they were looking at different things. King and Collins were looking at evidence in direct relation to their own existing services, and of course this evidence is powerful. Trenaman and Longland were looking at evidence of a different kind, in other situations and institutions, and in part they were looking at potential interest, which in many ways, and for differing reasons, fails to develop adequately with things as they are. These two kinds of evidence must always be remembered. It is very easy to think of the cultural level of a people as something single and something fixed. This is the trouble with phrases like 'the masses' and 'the great British public', which lead us to think not of actual people, living and growing in different ways, but of some large, many-headed thing with fixed habits. For the people Trenaman was talking about, there might be no registered evidence of actual participation in 'what we loosely call culture', while this goes on being identified with 'social and class differences'. But this identification is a product of history, and could change. For the children Longland was talking about, there is a critical passage from being a child to being an adult, and since for most of them the age of leaving school is about the age of becoming physically mature, they could not in any case go on with the same interests in quite the same way. But if the world of active education is identified with childhood, while the world of 'mass communications' is identified with the greater freedom of the adult, the personal choice is very difficult. Once again, however, this identification is a product of history, and could change. It is by no means necessary that the end of formal education should coincide with a critical stage of adolescence, thus often encouraging the idea that education is one of the childish things you put away.

Growth and change are central to this whole problem. But if you have a fixed idea about 'the masses', you cannot really take them into account. There is evidence that by taking an aspect of public taste, at a given time, and giving great publicity to it, you can make it more fixed, more emphatic, more important than it originally was. Dr Hilde Himmelweit, who directed the research published as *Television and the Child*, had this to say from the evidence of comparative studies over a period:

> It is liked, therefore its rating is high, therefore it is put on at peak viewing hours; and so the vicious circle is set up. I think one could very easily argue if one only looked at today's ratings – what can you expect? After all, people like Westerns, we put Westerns on. But because we have this trend study extending over a period of five years you can see that this kind of taste is to some extent – not of course entirely – an artificial one, a taste produced by the programme planners and producers.

It seems to be generally agreed that in the movement of public taste and opinion you cannot start a trend but you can accentuate one that exists. In the process, of course, you may be distorting the balance of interests and limiting the range of original potential response. If either of these things has happened, the evidence of public taste at any one time in relation to actually provided services cannot be taken as proving anything about people's needs and capacities.

In many known areas, a liking for certain kinds of thing already exists: this is where the trend starts from. But in a society like ours, changing in many ways, there are many unknown areas. Dr Silvey, while Head of B.B.C. Audience Research, said:

> The mass media do very largely confirm ideas which are already structured and held, but when it comes to spheres where there is a

great deal of confusion, you cannot reinforce something which is not there, and it is in those kinds of areas where I think responsibility is at its greatest.

This is very important, because in the new kinds of living that have been opening up to us, many of our ideas and our tastes are bound to be potential. If meeting these is not kept in balance with meeting the ideas and tastes we already have, which can be quickly and easily served, the whole process of growth and change is likely to be damaged.

Very few people would disagree with the argument that this situation requires great responsibility. King and Collins both mentioned their attempts to raise standards, and to create new interests. The important question is whether the organization and the ruling ideas of mass communications as we know them are adequate for this very difficult job.

I believe them to be inadequate, for these reasons. First, while we go on talking about 'the masses' we can have neither the respect for people nor the sense of growth that underlie responsibility. Second, while we go on thinking in a separatist way about 'classes' – whether social groupings or such educational groupings as 'the academic type', 'the technical type', 'the operative whose interests are all in his hands' – we cannot have sufficiently flexible ideas about people, and will be constantly tempted to divide our culture into separate areas with no bridges between them. Third, while there is an emphasis on profit, there will be a constant pressure to concentrate on things already known and safe, with never enough effort given to the much longer and more difficult job of trying new things and offering new ideas and experience. Fourth, while there is an emphasis on using the channels as a medium for advertising and selling, there will be a constant pressure to get people into 'the right frame of mind for buying', and to use the appeal of known tastes as a jumping-off ground for directing new interests and new opportunities into channels convenient to those with something ready to sell, but not necessarily relevant to the real problems of the new living itself.

The question of 'giving the public what it wants' has to be looked at, then, not by one rough-and-ready rule, but in this more general and varied way.

HIGH AND LOW

Men differ in their capacities for excellence. Yet democracy insists that everyone has an equal right to judge. Aren't we seeing, in our own time, the results of this contradiction? Isn't there great danger of the tradition of high culture being overwhelmed by mass culture, which expresses the tastes and standards of the ordinary man? Isn't it really our first duty to defend minority culture, which in its actual works is the highest achievement of humanity?

The difficulty here is that 'minority culture' can mean two things. It can mean the work of the great artists and thinkers, and of the many lesser but still important figures who sustain them. It can mean also the work of these men as received and used by a particular social minority, which will indeed often add to it certain works and habits of its own.

The great tradition is in many ways a common inheritance, and it has been the purpose of the best of modern education to make it as widely available as possible. Certainly this extension is never as easy as some people expect. Certainly it often happens that in the attempt to make difficult work more widely available, part of the value of the work is lost. Perhaps the whole attempt is wrongly conceived, and we should concentrate instead on maintaining the high tradition in its own terms.

The question is, however, can this in any case be done? The work of the great artists and thinkers has never been confined to their own company; it has always been made available to some others. And doesn't it often happen that those to whom it has been made available identify the tradition with themselves, grafting it into their own way of life? Thus, Sophocles, Shakespeare, Ibsen, Shaw, Rattigan may be a true succession, or it may not. The latest terms are always subject to error. Not every man under the towers of Oxford or Cambridge is the fellow of Cranmer, Newman, and Arnold, and these names cannot really be used to show that he is doing more important work, belongs more to the high tradition, than a teacher in a school at Croydon or a writer on the remote island of Jura. Yet, again and again, particular minorities confuse the superiority of the tradition which has been made available to them with their own superiority, an association which the passing of time or of frontiers can make suddenly ludicrous. We must always be careful to distinguish the great works of the past from the social minority which at a particular place and time identifies itself with them.

The great tradition very often continues itself in quite unexpected ways. Much new work, in the past, has been called 'low', in terms of the 'high' standards of the day. This happened to much of our Elizabethan drama, and to the novel in the eighteenth century. Looking back, we can understand this, because in each case the society was changing in fundamental ways. The minorities which assumed that they alone had the inheritance and guardianship of the great tradition in fact turned out to be wrong. This mistake can happen at any time. In our own century, there are such new forms as the film, the musical, and jazz. Each of these has been seen as 'low', a threat to 'our' standards. Yet during the period in which films have been made, there have been as many major contributions, in film, to the world's dramatic tradition, as there have been major plays. Of course most films are no where near this level. But from the past we have only the best work, and we can properly compare with this only our own best work. Some forms may well be better than others, in that they contain much greater possibilities for the artist, but this cannot be settled until there has been time for development. The great period of the novel came more than a century after the form had become popular and had been dismissed as 'low'. It realized possibilities which nobody could then have foreseen. The prestige of an old form is never decisive. There is no reason, today, why a science-fiction story should be thought less serious than an historical novel, or a new musical than a naturalist play. 'Low' equals 'unfamiliar' is one of the perennial cultural traps, and it is fallen into most easily by those who assume that in their own persons, in their own learned tastes and habits, they are the high tradition.

This might be agreed, but does it go to the real issue? These mistakes are made, but new minorities set them right. Still, however, they are minorities. Most people are not interested in the great tradition, old or new. Most people are not interested in art, but merely in entertainment. Actual popular taste is for such things as variety, the circus, sport, and processions. Why force art on such people, especially since you will be in danger of reducing art to that level, mixing it up with the popular and commercial worlds? Wouldn't your effort be better spent on maintaining real art for those who value it?

This distinction between art and entertainment may be much more difficult to maintain than it looks. At its extremes, of course, it is obvious. But over the whole range, is there any easy and absolute distinction? Great art can give us deep and lasting experiences, but the experience we get from many things that we rightly call art is quite often light and temporary. The excitement of the circus, the procession, the variety sketch, can be quite easily forgotten, but at the time it is often intense. Sport, in our century, has become a popular spectacle: its excitements again are intense and often temporary. There may be a difference between such things and the minor decorative arts, the passing comedies, the fashionable artistic performers, but can it really be seen as a difference between 'high' and 'low'? And even where the difference seems absolute, what follows from this? What has to be shown, to sustain the argument that 'high culture' is in danger of being overwhelmed by 'mass culture', is that there is not only difference but conflict. Most of us can test this in our own experience. For, in fact, we do not live in these neatly separated worlds. Many of us go one day to a circus, one day to a theatre; one day to the football, one day to a concert. The experiences are different, and vary widely in quality both between and within themselves. Do we in fact feel that our capacity for any one of these things is affected by our use of the others?

But perhaps this is not the main point. Isn't the real threat of 'mass culture' – of things like television rather than things like football or the circus – that it reduces us to an endlessly mixed, undiscriminating, fundamentally bored reaction? The spirit of everything, art and entertainment, can become so standardized that we have no absorbed interest in anything, but simply an indifferent acceptance, bringing together what Coleridge called 'indulgence of sloth and hatred of vacancy'. You're not exactly enjoying it, or paying any particular attention, but it's passing the time. And in so deadly an atmosphere the great tradition simply cannot live.

Most of us, I think, have experienced this atmosphere. At times, even, we take it as a kind of drug: in periods of tiredness or convalescence, or during tension and anxiety when we have to wait and when almost anything can help us to wait. Certainly as a normal habit of mind this would be enervating and dangerous; there is a lot of reality that we cannot afford to be cut off from, however much we may want some temporary relief.

The challenge of work that is really in the great tradition is that in many different ways it can get through with an intensity, a closeness, a concentration that in fact moves us to respond. It can be the reporter breaking through our prejudice to the facts; the dramatist reaching so deeply into our experience that we find it difficult, in the first shock, even to breathe; the painter suddenly showing us the shape of a street so clearly that we ask how we could ever have walked down it indifferently. It is sometimes a disturbing challenge to what we have always believed and done, and sometimes a way to new experience, new ways of seeing and feeling. Or again, in unexpected ways, it can confirm and strengthen us, giving new energy to what we already know is important, or what we knew but couldn't express.

Is this living world threatened by the routines of 'mass culture'? The threat is real, but it does not come only from 'mass culture'; it comes also from many kinds of routine art and routine thinking. There are many sources for the formula or routine which insulates us from reality. There is the weakness in ourselves, or at best the insufficient strength. There is also the intention of others, that we should be kept out of touch. Many interests are served by this kind of insulation: old forms of society, old and discredited beliefs, a wish to keep people quiet and uncritical. Such interests, based on power, habit, or privilege, are often served by, often actively seek, formulas and routines that insulate men from reality.

If we look at what we call 'mass culture' and 'minority culture', I am not sure that we invariably find one on the side of reality and one against it. Certainly the great works always challenge us with their own reality, and can stimulate us to active attention. But when these works are embedded in a particular minority culture, which adds to them not only its own local habits but also the facts and feelings which spring from its minority position, the effect can be very different. At best, a minority culture, in keeping the works available, offers the best that has been done and said in the world. At worst, it translates the best into its own accents, and confuses it with many other inferior things. I see no real evidence that it is a permanent and reliable means of maintaining a living excellence.

But even if it isn't permanent and reliable, isn't it bound to be better than the ordinary world of mass communications? There the construction of formulas seems almost built in. It is perhaps the only easy way of getting through quickly to a very large number of people, and the system seems to depend on this. Certainly we can only understand large-scale communications if we acknowledge the importance of formulas which can be fairly quickly and widely learned and used. Yet, in fact, formulas are necessary for all communication. What is at worst a formula for processing an experience is at best a convention for transmitting it in a widely available form. We have seen so much falsification, glamorization, and real vulgarization that we often forget how many facts, how many new opinions, how many new kinds of work and new ways of seeing the world nevertheless get through. By comparison with times when there was no highly organized communications system these are dramatic gains. We have then to adjust the balance much more carefully than a simple contrast of 'minority' and 'mass', 'high' and 'low' would suggest.

There is one further argument, that can very easily be overlooked. The great tradition is itself always in danger of being vulgarized when it is confined to a minority culture. Just because it is a mixed inheritance, from many societies and many times as well as from many kinds of men, it cannot easily be contained within one limited social form. Further, if it is so contained, there can be deep and unnecessary hostility to it from those outside the social minority. If the great tradition is not made generally available, there is often this frightening combination of hostility and a vacuum. What then usually happens is that this is penetrated and exploited from outside. In the worst cultural products of our time, we find little that is genuinely popular, developed from the life of actual communities. We find instead a synthetic culture, or anti-culture, which is alien to almost everybody, persistently hostile to art and intellectual activity, which it spends much of its time in misrepresenting, and given over to exploiting indifference, lack of feeling, frustration, and hatred. It finds such common human interests as sex, and turns them into crude caricatures or glossy facsimiles. It plays repeatedly around hatred and aggression, which it never discharges but continually feeds. This is not the culture of 'the ordinary man'; it is the culture of the disinherited. It seems to me that those who have contrived the disinheritance, by artificially isolating the great tradition, bear as heavy a responsibility for these destructive elements as their actual providers.

In Britain, we have to notice that much of this bad work is American in origin. At certain levels, we are culturally an American colony. But of course it is not the best American culture that we are getting, and the import and imitation of the worst has been done, again and again, by some of our own people, significantly often driven by hatred or envy of the English minority which has associated the great tradition with itself. To go pseudo-American is a way out of the English complex of class and culture, but of course it solves nothing; it merely ritualizes the emptiness and despair. Most bad culture is the result of this kind of social collapse. The genuinely popular tradition is despised, the great tradition is kept exclusive, and into the gap pour the speculators who know how to exploit disinheritance because they themselves are rooted in nothing.

The general situation is very difficult to understand. In part, now, the great tradition is being responsibly extended, and is finding an excellent response, both in the real increase of audiences, and in the answering vitality of new contributions to it from new kinds of experience. The purely destructive exploitation of the vacuum is also very powerful, in part because the control of our cultural organization has passed very largely into the hands of men who know no other definitions. At the same time, against all the apparent odds, elements of the really popular tradition persist, especially in variety, sport, some kinds of spectacle, and the impulse to make our own entertainment, especially in music. It seems impossible to understand this many-sided and constantly changing situation through the old formulas of 'minority' and 'mass', which are the symptoms of the collapse rather than keys to understanding it. We have to look at a new situation in new ways.

VIOLENCE AND VALUES

Is there too much emphasis, in the popular Sunday newspapers, in television drama, and in the production and advertising of films, on 'violence' and 'sex'? That the emphasis is there can hardly be denied. But what kind of emphasis is it, and what are its actual or probable effects?

Who knows?

A fair amount of research has been carried out, in some fields, particularly in relation to 'violence'. Three kinds of question have been asked. How many items involving violence appear, as a proportion of total output? What attitudes to violence appear in these items? Are there cases where the apparent moral attitude is contradicted by the actual presentation?

The first question is easily answered, though it has never been looked at in a continuous way and over the whole communications field. There have been such counts as that of 7,065 acts or threats of violence on the television programmes of New York City in one week. In Britain a count of programmes on television, by the Council for Children's Welfare in a sample week, showed the following:

Family viewing hours (6–9 p.m.)	: 21 hours
I.T.V. 'crime' and 'Westerns'	: 5½ hours
B.B.C. 'crime' and 'Westerns'	: 2¼ hours

Some later figures (1965), for programmes involving crime and violence, in the whole schedules offered, were:

B.B.C. 1	: 6 hours	5 minutes
I.T.V.	: 6 hours	35 minutes
B.B.C. 2	: 4 hours	20 minutes

These amounted to some eleven per cent (B.B.C. 1), eleven per cent (I.T.V.) and thirteen per cent (B.B.C. 2), of all material shown. Of the hours stated, the following were in family viewing periods (6–9 p.m. weekdays, weekend afternoons and early evenings): B.B.C. 1, 4¼ hours; I.T.V., 2¾ hours; B.B.C. 2, 2½ hours.

It is important to know such figures, but they are sometimes difficult to interpret. It is often argued that it is not the appearance of violence that matters, but the attitude to it within the work. On the other hand, the place of any one theme, however handled, within the general distribution of interests in the culture as a whole, is surely also important. Simple 'quantity counts' can be useful in showing this distribution of interests. If it is argued, for example, that 'violence ought to appear because it is a part of real life', it is relevant to ask its proportion in real life as compared with its proportion in newspapers, films, and television programmes. Any count in our own society would show that the proportion in communications is much higher than the proportion in the rest of our living. We should then ask not only why this is so, but what other interests are reduced or excluded to allow this altered proportion.

The second question, on attitudes to violence, has produced some detailed work. The most useful is that recorded in *Television and the Child*. There, for example, the difference between 'Westerns' and 'crime plays' is defined as a difference between stylization and black-and-white simplicity in the former, complexity and 'realism' in the latter. In moral attitudes, 'the central lesson of Westerns is that good triumphs over bad through violence – the manly, as well as the only, course of action. The villain's case is never stated, no sympathy is invited for him, and the hero never gains anything from his deeds. There is no suggestion of internal conflict or indecision.' In crime stories, there are three kinds of explicit values: 'First, that crime does not pay, because the law has vast resources. ... Second, that the activities of criminals and the law are not in fact dissimilar. Both sides bully and cheat if necessary. ... Third, that appearances are deceptive; a person may look harmless and yet be a criminal (though hardly ever the other way round). ... Man is often not responsible for his deeds ... he cannot help himself. While the law must be upheld, the criminal can yet evoke sympathy.' A further general difference between 'Westerns' and 'crime plays' is that in the former 'the impact of violence is dulled because there are no close-ups at the kill and also because the emphasis is on opposing sides rather than individuals'. In crime plays 'there is no attempt to evade the consequences of violence, the camera stays with a man who has been hit; we see blood on his hands and beads of sweat on his face ... detailed expressions of physical pain'.

The third question, on possible differences between explicit attitudes and those actually embodied, has been too little studied. Yet it is important because the argument about effects can become naïve if only the formal 'moral' or 'lesson' is looked at. Thus, the regular message of crime plays that 'crime does not pay' may in fact be begging the question of what 'paying' really is. That the criminal is caught may be one conclusion. That in the process of his crime there has been 'pay' and satisfaction may often be another. The whole moral effect can then be deeply confused. On disturbing human themes, it is possible and even probable that there will often be conflict between the formal moral ending or moral intention and the actual experience most strongly expressed. Thus analysis of an American film against racial prejudice found that 'fantasies from a less conscious level come to the surface', expressing deep prejudices in a powerful way and making the effect of the whole film ambiguous.*

There is controversy over the results of these various kinds of content analysis. There is even more controversy over the effects of the content itself. Thus Noel Stevenson, of Independent Television, said:

We have been talking about things like violence and immorality. As soon as you suggest that television can make people violent or make them immoral you are at once dealing with an area of values on which there are enormous social pressures – our home, our neighbourhood, our religious groups, our industrial groups – all, virtually speaking, are against violence, against immorality. I think myself that television has very little effect in any of these fields.

Dr Mark Abrams, sociologist, said:

The abundance of this noxious material in the mass media is beyond dispute. But does it lead to direct, imitative behaviour on the part of ordinary average children? . . . Does it create among them a

* *Audio-Visual Communication Review*, Gerbner, Vol. 6, No. 2, Spring, 1958.

general climate of undesirable values? The available evidence from research on these points among children is slight and often negative. It appears that when maladjusted and well-adjusted children are exposed to identical amounts of violent mass-media content, the former, unlike the latter, show a marked preference for such material, derive distinctive satisfactions from it, and, in the process of consumption, their problems are sustained rather than resolved. Since media violence, in some way as yet unknown to us, apparently intensifies the difficulties of maladjusted and frustrated children, a strong case can be made out for removing such material. The strength of the case, however, depends very largely on two considerations: first, how large is the proportion of our children who are maladjusted and frustrated? If is it very low, e.g., 1 or 2 per cent, then the introduction of censorship could hardly be justified; while if it is high, e.g., 20 or 25 per cent, then the case would seem to be unanswerable. Unfortunately, this is yet another area where, in spite of the abundance of debate, we lack any reliable, relevant facts. We do not know whether it is 2 per cent or 22 per cent.

Dr Hilde Himmelweit, psychologist, said:

If, year after year, one gives children a diet in which these elements feature rather largely . . . there is no question that their view of society, that violence is a rather ordinary thing, that conflicts can best be solved by physical violence, may gradually make an impact on the children. I would have thought this was not a risk worth taking.

Who cares?

The question is not only 'who knows?' It is also 'who cares?' To prove the effects of any particular kind of work is difficult, if not impossible, because anyone exposed to that work will also have been exposed to a whole range of other experience, from which the effects of the work itself cannot easily be separated. At the same time, this difficulty applies to almost everything that society seeks to control or forbid or encourage. In the end, decisions of this kind are made either from

the standards of a ruling group, or from the general conscience of the society, which may often have been aroused by
a crusading minority. It is important that allegations of
danger, or possible danger, should be critically examined in
the light of the best knowledge we have. But it is wrong to
suppose that the only argument now current is that between
people who make different estimates of this kind of risk.
Behind this argument is another body of opinion, which is
not thinking in these terms at all. The proprietors and editors
of popular Sunday newspapers and comics, the publishers
and authors of 'sex-and-violence' novels, the controllers and
producers of similar television programmes, the producers
and advertisers of similar films, do not base their activity on
an estimate of the danger of their work to the public and,
having found it non-existent or negligible, go ahead. Their
principle is the quite different one that if such work will sell
or is popular it is all right to provide it. It is here that the
second question arises: who cares?

The whole argument would be easier if those who do care
were all of the same kind. Through all the differences of
interpretation, there is a similar kind of concern among
teachers, among many parents, among social welfare bodies,
and among sociologists, psychologists, and writers. But over-
lapping their arguments, and sometimes resembling them,
are the complaints of those who are judging one generation
by the standards of another, who ask 'My Lords, where are
we going?' or 'What on earth are we coming to, in this
degraded modern world?' The confusion was interestingly
illustrated by the argument about the publication of *Lady
Chatterley's Lover*. This was a fore-runner of the whole current
discussion.

For some people, at one extreme, the argument was
simple: 'Let us get rid of these old-fashioned restrictions, this
self-punishing Puritanism. People should be able to read

what they want to, and artists of course must be free to write what they want to.' For others, at the opposite extreme, the argument was also simple: 'The Christian virtues of our children are being violated in order to fill the ever-bulging pockets of unscrupulous publishers with gold filched from the virtues of our children.' *Lady Chatterley's Lover* was seen as of a piece with cheap pornography, suggestive films, horror-comics, and violence on television.

The more difficult position was that of people who used one argument – 'the artist's freedom to publish' – in defence of Lawrence, and another argument – 'the duty of society to protect the immature' – in criticism of the Sunday news-papers and television violence. I do not really see how both these arguments can be honestly used. I am sure that *Lady Chatterley's Lover* is in a wholly different class, as art, from the great bulk of popular work. I am sure also, in my own mind, that it would do good where other work does harm. But, as a matter of general principle, we cannot rely on absolute con-trasts between good and bad work; there will always be work that is mixed or intermediate. If we stand on 'freedom to publish', we shall not in fact be able to confine this to moral masterpieces. If we stand on 'protecting the immature', we shall have to accept that in fact all work, good, bad, and indifferent, will have to undergo this scrutiny. It is argued that effect can be judged in terms of the kind of audience addressed: something all right for adults would be wrong for children. This may be generally true, but in practice it seems that it is impossible to confine most work to any one group: whatever the intention, the actual audiences to some extent overlap, quite apart from the natural overlap of adolescence. Moreover, within each audience, whether of adults, adolescents, or children, there will be wide differences of character and stability which may have everything to do with the actual effect. A psychopathic adult may be more easily affected, and may as a result do more damage, than a very young but secure child.

We need more evidence on this whole question; we always need more evidence. But is it always sensible, if a matter is urgent, to go on waiting for more evidence, and, if so, for how long? Action is in any case already being taken: many things are being distributed, many things are being banned or clipped. The real questions seem to be: Who makes the decisions, to distribute or to ban? On what grounds are these made or publicly justified? It may be very difficult to find the best possible system, either in institutions or in values, but, as Carlyle said, 'If you ask which is the worst, I answer, this which we now have, that chaos should sit umpire in it; this is the worst.' For we have evidently not made up our minds between the competing cries, 'freedom to publish', 'duty to be responsible', 'what's wanted should be provided', 'perversion or confusion of our values'. Until we are clear about this, and have some real principles and procedures, which we are prepared to recognize over the whole field, the chaos, and any possible damage, will continue.

THE CONTRIBUTORS

Surely the people who really matter, in any culture, are the active contributors. Why do we talk always about publics and audiences and cultural systems? Surely the only way to get good culture is to have good artists and performers. And is there really anything we can do about getting them? Perhaps the most we can do is to try to create a society in which artists find it worth living.

Certainly the contributors are of the first importance. But can we really assume that they are all of the same kind, with the same general needs? And can we also assume that different publics and systems have no effect on the sort of contributors we actually get?

We can distinguish four main kinds of contributor: the creative artist, the performer, the reporter, the commentator or reviewer. Each of these has, in the first instance, a direct responsibility to his work. It is true that each is trying to communicate this work to others. It is obviously desirable that each should try to make this communication as successful as possible. But, in the act of work itself, there is a special kind of responsibility. To understand this we have to look more closely at what communication involves.

A reporter gets at certain facts. A commentator or reviewer gives his opinion of an actual event or work. A performer expresses, in his own medium, a work created by himself or another. A creative artist seeks to embody in a work his own experience or vision. Each sees his work differently, but certain factors are common. Each, including the artist, is trying to put his work into a communicable form. Yet each can only communicate, with any real satisfaction, on the basis of what he actually finds necessary to say or show. It is no use thinking 'If I altered it, they would understand it more easily', because while it might then be easier to get in touch with others, it might no longer be getting in touch on the basis of what actually needs to be said.

This reality defines the freedom of cultural contribution. In their different ways, the reporter, the commentator and reviewer, the performer, and the artist need a guaranteed freedom to communicate what, in terms of *their own* understanding of their work, needs to be communicated. This sounds like, and is, a definition of individual freedom. But it is not only for the sake of individuals that this freedom should be guaranteed. A good society depends on the free availability of facts and opinions, and on the growth of vision and consciousness – the articulation of what men have actually seen and known and felt. Any restriction of the freedom of individual contribution is actually a restriction of the resources of the society.

How is the communication actually achieved? It depends, of course, either on a common language or on known conventions, or at least on the beginnings of these. If the common language and the conventions exist, the contributor tries to use them as well as he can. But often, especially with original artists and thinkers, the problem is in one way that of creating a language, or creating a convention, or at least of developing the language and conventions to the point where they are capable of bearing his precise meaning. In literature, in music, in the visual arts, in the sciences, in social thinking, in philosophy, this kind of development has occurred again and again. It often takes a long time to get through, and for many people it will remain difficult. But we need never think that it is impossible; creative energy is much more powerful than we sometimes suppose. While any man is engaged in this struggle to say new things in new ways, he is usually more than ever concentrated on the actual work, and not on its possible audience. Many artists and scientists share this fundamental unconcern about the ways in which their work will be received. They may be glad if it is understood and appreciated, hurt if it is not, but while the work is being done there can be no argument. The thing has to come out as the man himself sees it.

In this sense it is true that it is the duty of society to create conditions in which such men can live. For whatever the value of any individual contribution, the general body of work is of immense value to everyone. But of course things are not so formal, in reality. There is not society on the one hand and these individuals on the other. In ordinary living, and in his work, the contributor shares in the life of his society, which often affects him both in minor ways and in ways sometimes so deep that he is not even aware of them. His ability to make his work public depends on the actual communication system: the language itself, or certain visual or musical or scientific conventions, and the institutions through which the communication will be passed. The effect of these on his actual work can be almost infinitely variable. For it is not only a communication system outside him; it is also, however original he may be, a communication system which is in fact part of himself. Many contributors make active use of this kind of internal communication system. It is to themselves, in a way, that they first show their conceptions, play their music, present their arguments. Not only as a way of getting these clear, in the process of almost endless testing that active composition involves. But also, whether consciously or not, as a way of putting the experience into a communicable form. If one mind has grasped it, even if only the mind that also created it, then it may be open to other minds.

In this deep sense, the society is in some ways already present in the act of composition. This is always very difficult to understand, but often, when we have the advantage of looking back at a period, we can see, even if we cannot explain, how this was so. We can see how much even highly original individuals had in common, in their actual work, and in what is called their 'structure of feeling', with other individual workers of the time, and with the society of that time to which they belonged. The historian is also continually struck by the fact that men of this kind felt isolated at the very time when in reality they were beginning to get through. This can also be noticed in our own time, when some of the most deeply influential men feel isolated and even rejected. The society and the communication are there, but it is difficult to recognize them, difficult to be sure.

When we turn to institutions, we need to remember this deep social reality of communication. For if we do not, we can be easily tempted into one of two very common false positions. Either we can say that we should leave the contributors alone, because they are so important: a form of flattery which in fact comes through as neglect, leaving men already at the limits of their strength to the doubtful mercy of every wind that blows. The contributors are involved in their society, both in profound ways and in their ordinary human needs, and they usually suffer if they are cut off from it, whether as 'impractical dreamers' or as 'untouchable spirits'. Or we can say, as so many now do, that the institutions of communication should be defined first, and then the contributors fitted into them. We have seen this happen so often that it is sometimes the only danger we are aware of. It is certainly a constant and serious danger. Power can say to the reporter: 'Remember what kind of paper this is; if you want to work on it, learn its ways.' Or to the commentator and reviewer: 'Remember on what *beliefs* this society is based; express your opinion by all means, but of course within these beliefs.' Or to the performer: 'What in fact we like to see is this; you're a talented person, you could surely learn.' Or to the artist: 'Of course creative people are a bit temperamental, they get wrapped up in themselves, but think of the good you could do, think of the people you could reach, if you did this and not that.' Many contributors, of course, will do as they are told. Some, though, will cry from the depths: 'Leave me alone, let me get on with my work.' And then, in the next breath, paradoxically: 'Why are the really creative people always ignored and neglected?'

Is there any way between these opposite errors? Well, there is a clear difference between those contributors who cannot work at all without institutions (film and television companies, theatres, orchestras, newspapers, and magazines), and those who are not so immediately dependent (writers, composers, painters, sculptors), though in the end institutions affect them. In each of these kinds, there are many who compromise early: learning to produce exactly what the institution wants, or learning how to satisfy the market. The pressures are often so great, in the absence of any alternative policy, that this seems bound to happen in very many cases. Of those who stand out for their own work, those least immediately dependent are obviously in the stronger position, and their view of the matter is often received with impatience by those who cannot even work unless an institution is found. Nevertheless, they have kept alive a principle which is of general importance. However arrogant it sounds in particular cases, especially when made by one man on behalf of his own work, it remains true that a contributor's freedom to work on his own terms is a gain to society as a whole. The only useful institutions, in cultural organization, are those which are designed to guarantee this freedom. Such arrangements will vary according to the work, and in the case of those contributors not immediately dependent on institutions, the more informal they are the better. But in other cases, and even for the most individual contributors, institutions of a kind will in any case be there. Behind the proclamation of the freedom of the reporter and the artist, real freedom, in many cases, has dramatically declined, as official and commercial organization has become tighter and more pervasive. It is no longer useful merely to proclaim this freedom. What matters is to work out its practical means. In this, the contributors need the support of the wider public. I do not think this support will be gained, in practice (it is gained without difficulty in theory, which costs nothing), unless the arguments for freedom of contribution are put on a wider basis. Simply saying 'leave me alone' may produce exactly that result: the nonconformists will be left alone, while the conformists take over the whole culture. Yet, if we understand the real process of communication, the contributor's freedom and his need for control over his own resources can be reasonably seen as a means to freedom in the whole society, and as the best way in which the contributor can serve the society. From the freedom of the contributor, properly understood, can spring the real relations with society on which he also depends.

We might usefully remember some words of Blake. He suffered through most of his life from neglect and the vagaries of the market, and he was a profoundly original poet and artist. He seems to me to have cut through a world of fashionable cant with this direct and wise conclusion:

> Some People & not a few Artists have asserted that the Painter of this Picture would not have done so well if he had been properly Encourag'd. Let those who think so, reflect on the State of Nations under Poverty & their incapability of Art; tho' Art is above either, the Argument is better for Affluence than Poverty; & tho' he would not have been a greater Artist, yet he would have produced Greater works of Art in proportion to his means.

THE SYSTEMS

Perhaps it comes down to this: either the communication system is controlled or it is free. In a democracy there can be no argument on this point: the system must be free or there is no democracy. In a free system many of the things produced may be bad or offensive, or may seem bad and offensive to some people. But the only alternative is a controlled system, or monopoly, in which some people are imposing their tastes on others. 'In fact,' said Sir Robert Fraser, then Head of the Independent Television Authority, defending the introduction of commercial television, 'the old system of monopoly in Britain was carried away by a wave of democratic thought and feeling.'

It would be easy to score debating points against Sir Robert Fraser: to ask, for example, what 'a wave of democratic thought and feeling' has in common with the actual process of pressure-group lobbying, much of it by persons with a direct financial interest, which got commercial television through. But this is not the main issue, since behind all the detail of contemporary controversy lies an evident conflict of principles, which has to be faced and understood.

In one way, the basic choice is between control and freedom, but in actual terms it is more often a choice between a measure of control and a measure of freedom, and the substantial argument is about how these can be combined. Further, the bare words 'controlled' and 'free' do not seem sufficiently precise, in themselves, to describe the kinds of communication system which we have had or known about or wanted. I believe that we can distinguish four main kinds, and that to describe and compare these will make our thinking about control and freedom more realistic. The four kinds are: authoritarian, paternal, commercial, and democratic.

Authoritarian

In this system, communications are seen as part of the total machine through which a minority governs a society. The first purpose of communication is to transmit the instructions, ideas, and attitudes of the ruling group. As a matter of policy, alternative instructions, ideas, and attitudes are excluded. Monopoly of the means of communication is a necessary part of the whole political system: only certain printers, publishing houses, newspapers, theatres, broadcasting stations will be allowed. Sometimes these will be directly controlled by the ruling group, who will then directly decide what is transmitted. At other times, a more indirect control will be completed by a system of censorship, and often by a system of political and administrative action against sources unfavourable to those in power.

Such a system can operate with varying degrees of severity,

and in the interest of several different kinds of society. We can see it in past periods in Britain as clearly as in modern totalitarian states. The distinguishing characteristic of such a system is that the purpose of communication is to protect, maintain, or advance a social order based on minority power.

Paternal

A paternal system is an authoritarian system with a conscience: that is to say, with values and purposes beyond the maintenance of its own power. Authoritarians, on various grounds, claim the right to rule. In a paternal system, what is asserted is the duty to protect and guide. This involves the exercise of control, but it is a control directed towards the development of the majority in ways thought desirable by the minority. If monopoly of the means of communication is used, it is argued that this is to prevent the means being abused by groups which are destructive or evil. Censorship is widely used, in such a system, both directly and indirectly, but it is defended on the grounds that certain groups and individuals need, in their own interest and in the public interest, protection against certain kinds of art or ideas which would be harmful to them. Where the authoritarian system transmits orders, and the ideas and attitudes which will promote their acceptance, the paternal system transmits values, habits, and tastes, which are its own justification as a ruling minority, and which it wishes to extend to the people as a whole. Criticism of such values, habits, and tastes will be seen as at best a kind of rawness and inexperience, at worst a moral insurrection against a tried and trusted way of life. The controllers of a paternal system see themselves as guardians. Though patient, they must be uncompromising in defence of their central values. At the same time, the proper discharge of their duty requires a high sense of responsibility and seriousness. At different times, and serving different social orders, the paternal system can vary in the degree to which it explicitly announces its role or explains its methods. The actual methods can also vary widely: sometimes putting the blanket over everything; sometimes allowing a measure of controlled dissent or tolerance as a safety-valve. But the general purpose and atmosphere of the system remain unmistakable.

Commercial

The commercial attitude to communications is powerfully opposed to both authoritarianism and paternalism. Instead of communication being for government or for guidance, it is argued that men have the right to offer for sale any kind of work, and that all men have the right to buy any kind that is offered. In this way, it is claimed, the freedom of communication is assured. You do not have to ask anybody's leave to publish or to read. Works are openly offered for sale and openly bought, as people actually choose.

In its early stages, and in some of its later stages, such a system is certainly a means to freedom by comparison with either of the former systems. But since this freedom depends on the market it can run into difficulties. Can a work be offered for sale if there is no certainty that people will in fact buy it? When production is cheap, this risk will often be taken. When production is expensive, it may not be. In a modern system of communications many kinds of production are inevitably expensive. What, then, happens to the simple original principle? First: works whose sale is uncertain, or likely to be very small in relation to cost, may not be offered at all. Second: speed of sale becomes an important factor – it is not easy to wait for years for a return on a large investment if the act of buying and selling is the most important consideration. Investment elsewhere might bring much quicker returns. Third: if the amount of capital needed to finance a work is large, there can be no free offering for sale, as in the original principle. Individual artists will almost certainly not possess the necessary capital. They have then to be financed by individuals or groups with such capital, and it is probable that considerations of extent or speed of sale, and so of return or profit on the investment, will be decisive as to whether such an offer of financing is made. But then practical control of the means of communication, over large areas and particularly in the more expensive kinds, can pass to individuals or groups whose main, if not only, qualification will be that they possess or can raise the necessary capital. Such groups, by the fact of this qualification, will often be quite unrepresentative of the society as a whole; they will be, in fact, a minority within it. Thus the control claimed as a matter of power by authoritarians, and as a matter of principle by paternalists, is often achieved as a matter of practice in the operation of the commercial system. Anything can be said, provided that you can afford to say it and that you can say it profitably.

Democratic

We have experienced the other three systems, but the democratic system, in any full sense, we can only discuss and imagine. It shares with the early commercial system a definition of communication which insists that all men have the right to offer what they choose and to receive what they choose. It is firmly against authoritarian control of what can be said, and against paternal control of what ought to be said. But also it is against commercial control of what can profitably be said, because this also can be a tyranny.

All proposals for new systems appear abstract, and at times unconvincing, because it is only when they are put into practice that they can be felt to be real. The working out of any democratic system will obviously be long and difficult, but what matters first is to define the general nature of a cultural system compatible with democracy, since there is only any chance of success in building it if enough of us can agree that this is the kind of thing we want.

There are two related considerations: the right to transmit and the right to receive. It must be the basis of any democratic culture, first, that these are basic rights; second, that they can never be tampered with by minorities; third, that if they are ever in any way limited, by some majority decision of the society, this can happen only after open and adequate public discussion, to which all are free to contribute and which will remain open to challenge and review.

On the right to transmit, the basic principle of democracy is that since all are full members of the society, all have the right to speak as they wish or find. This is not only an individual right, but a social need, since democracy depends on the active participation and the free contribution of all its members. The right to receive is complementary to this: it is the means of participation and of common discussion.

The institutions necessary to guarantee these freedoms must clearly be of a public-service kind, but it is very important that the idea of public service should not be used as a cover for a paternal or even authoritarian system. The idea of public service must be detached from the idea of public monopoly, yet remain public service in the true sense. The only way of achieving this is to create new kinds of institution.

The principle should be that the active contributors have control of their own means of expression. In the case of contributors not immediately dependent on institutions, this means guaranteeing them, if they want, certain facilities which will be their means of living and working. In cases where the work can only be done through institutions, it means creating the opportunity for the setting up, by various working groups, of their own companies, which will then be guaranteed the facilities they need. Some of these guarantees can be given by various intermediate institutions, themselves not dependent or directly dependent on the organs of government. But probably the greater part of the necessary resources will have to come directly from public funds. It is then necessary to create intermediate bodies, including representatives of the public and of the companies, to hold these public resources in trust for the society as a whole and for the needs of the various companies.

There should be no direct control by government over contributors. The creation of intermediate bodies, and of a contractual system by which individuals and companies are guaranteed certain resources for the work they want to do, can in practice make governmental control impossible, so long as the general life of the society remains democratic. In any system, if general democracy goes, cultural democracy will go too. But while there is general democracy (in defence of which an active cultural democracy is continually necessary) what matters most is a clear acceptance of the principle that the resources exist for the contributors to use for the work they themselves want to do, and that all decisions about the actual allocation of resources should be publicly argued and open to challenge and review.

There are two difficulties in this principle, certain also to be difficult in practice. The case for control by the contributors is that the society cannot by any means be better served than by giving the contributors their freedom and the necessary resources to work with. Control by functionless financial groups, or by political or administrative factions, is certain to be damaging. But will there, can there be no control at all: either by the allocation of resources to this work rather than that, or by any measures thought generally necessary to protect the public interest?

A democratic culture would need to allot considerable resources, to keep the first danger small. It would need in any case to resist any tendency to restrict work to its own channels, however adequate. If, even in the most enlightened system, an individual or a group cannot get support, it must be quite clear that there is nothing to stop them working in any way they can, and offering their work in any way they can: a situation in which they would be much as now. The more difficult aspect of this question is that a healthy culture depends on growth, yet at any given moment new kinds of work may command little interest, and there might be considerable public pressure to give them little or no support. How can this be overcome, in any democratic way? There is no simple answer, and the only possible answer is that if it is of the nature of democratic culture that it keeps the channels of growth clear, it is a public duty to see that individuals or groups offering new kinds of work are given at least a fair chance. The problem is really one of holding the ring, to give new work the time (it will often be a long time) to prove itself. The more varied the organization, the more independent companies there are, the more this chance is likely to be given.

The second difficulty is severe. We have seen how in certain cases it can be deeply held that there are certain things which ought not to be offered, because they are likely, on the available evidence, to harm people. Will not such restrictions have to be made? Even if they are publicly argued, publicly decided, and continually open to review, are they not still restrictions? Is not paternalism in some form necessary after all? In fact, of course, if it is a majority decision it is not paternalism. But it will still feel like it, to those affected. Again, there is no simple answer to this. The general issues, and all particular cases, need continual discussion. I believe that with the pressure of profit lifted there would be less work

of this difficult kind. Yet there would always be some, and
you might get a majority decision against serious work. The
only way to prevent this is to promote the most open discussion, including the contributor's own reasoning, or
reasoning on his behalf. I do not believe that, when this is
done, people usually choose wrongly. In any event, one case
lost is often the next case won, for in arguing the cases there
is a real growth of understanding.

It seems to be best to let the contribution be made, and let
the contributor take responsibility for it. The curious situation now, in a commercial culture, is that the contributor is
often neither free nor responsible: neither doing what he
would independently have done, nor answerable to public
criticism for what he has actually done. The balance inherent
in democracy requires the creation of both these new conditions: freedom to do and freedom to answer, as an active
process between many individuals.

SUMMARY

The four systems described, authoritarian, paternal, commercial, and democratic, are all to some extent active, in
practice or in local experiment, in contemporary Britain.
The vestiges of authoritarianism are there, in certain kinds
of censorship; the first experiments in democracy are also
there, in local ways. But the main struggle, over the last
generation, has been between the paternal and commercial
systems, and it is clear that the commercial has been
steadily winning. It is most important, in this situation,
that we should not confine the debate to the limited contrast
of 'controlled' and 'free' systems, but instead should look
over the whole range, and into detailed comparisons and
possibilities.

CHAPTER FIVE

PROPOSALS

WHAT can be done? Should anything be done? We must answer these questions for ourselves, but in fact, if some of us decide to do nothing, this does not mean that the situation will stay as it is. No social process, in contemporary Britain, is more dynamic than this extension of communications. This means that there will in any case be further change, some of it of a very rapid and far-reaching kind. It may all seem too complicated or too powerful to touch. Or it may seem, on balance, to be going reasonably well, with such faults as there are so intractable that any attempt at cure might be worse than the disease. In any case, all possible courses of action have different motives: no action in this field is separate from action in the society as a whole, where there are deep and important disagreements. If we act, or try to act, we must state our reasons and our motives.

I stated my own position in *The Long Revolution*. I see this cultural revolution as part of a great process of human liberation, comparable in importance with the industrial revolution and the struggle for democracy. I want this process to continue, and I have no desire at all to go back, or try to go back, to any earlier stage of its history. I believe also that we must not see any part of this great process of change as separate, or as an end in itself. For, if we do, we run into contradictions of a severe kind – setting cultural difficulties against democracy, or setting cultural and democratic values against the industrial revolution. The essential values, as I see them, are common to the whole process: that men should grow in capacity and power to direct their own lives – by creating democratic institutions, by bringing new sources of energy to human work, and by extending the expression and exchange of experience on which understanding depends.

Different societies will pursue these aims in different ways. In Britain, we start with a tradition which already, at its best, is firmly attached to this kind of progress. The aim has been there, in many minds, for several generations: to create an educated and participating democracy. We can achieve this only in terms of an advanced industrial society, and the community we are building is and must be a wholly new kind of community, in which the new kinds of communication – not only television and broadcasting and cheap books, but also greater mobility and greater opportunities to travel – must be not only taken into account, but welcomed. The growth of large-scale organization and communication is a major human gain, far outweighing the real difficulties and confusions it has also brought, and this extension needs to go much farther yet, towards a world community. Any action we take, then, should be in line with these aims. And we shall understand the whole process much better if we grasp it as part of a long and now almost universal historical movement, in which even in an advanced society like Britain we are still at a comparatively early stage.

In the stress of change there is a great deal of confusion. It is often argued that we can only meet this with an even greater emphasis on personal responsibility. This is true, provided we recognize that responsibility, in any real sense, is in any case continually changing. Indeed, part of the meaning of responsibility is the capacity to recognize and respond to new situations. What is often meant, however, by this emphasis on personal responsibility, is that we should not do anything very much in the way of public change, because that is comparatively superficial, whereas if parents could only be responsible ('let them use the freedom of the switch') there would be real strength. This is a tragic underestimate of the situation when it is seriously offered, and a simple evasion of responsibility when it is ordinarily offered. Personal choice is real and necessary, but for just this reason we cannot really choose for others. Even parents cannot, and in my view ought not to, choose in this absolute way for their children. The burden of wise choice needs an extension of responsibility in which we can all share. If we want to make the best of the new and real opportunities which cultural extension provides, and if we want to avoid and put right the mistakes which are in fact being made, personal responsibility has to grow into public responsibility, which is a different and absolutely radical thing.

What forms can this public responsibility take? First, in education, we can find new ways of developing the capacity for personal and independent response and choice. Second, in amendment of institutions, and in legislation, we can make sure that our cultural organization is, in real ways, responsible to the society of which it is so important a part. Third, in new social construction, we can propose and try to get agreement for radical changes in institutions, to make them adequate to the needs of a growing society.

I am setting down certain proposals in each of these three fields. All need further discussion, and are offered for discussion.

IN EDUCATION

We already teach communication, in certain ways, and we also teach some practice and appreciation of the arts. Some of this work is good, but some of it is limited by assumptions taken over from old-fashioned ideas of culture and society, and some of it is even harmful.

Teaching speech

At the roots of much of our cultural thinking is our actual
experience of speech. In Britain the question of good speech
is deeply confused, and is in itself a major source of many of
the divisions in our culture. It is inevitable, in modern society,
that our regional speech-forms should move closer to each
other, and that many extreme forms should disappear. But
this should be a natural process, as people move and travel
and meet more freely, and as they hear different speakers in
films, television, and broadcasting. The mistake is to assume
that there is already a 'correct' form of modern English
speech, which can serve as a standard to condemn all others.
In fact 'public-school English', in the form in which many
have tried to fix it, cannot now become a common speech-
form in the country as a whole: both because of the social
distinctions now associated with its use, and because of the
powerful influence of American speech-forms. Yet many
good forms of modified regional speech are in practice emerging and extending. The barriers imposed by dialect are
reduced, in these forms, without the artificiality of imitating
a form remote from most people's natural speaking. This is
the path of growth. Yet in much speech training, in schools,
we go on assuming that there is already one 'correct' form
over the country as a whole. Thousands of us are made to
listen to our natural speaking with the implication from the
beginning that it is *wrong*. This sets up such deep tensions,
such active feelings of shame and resentment, that it should
be no surprise that we cannot discuss culture in Britain
without at once encountering tensions and prejudices deriv-
ing from this situation. If we experience speech training as
an aspect of our social inferiority, a fundamental cultural
division gets built in, very near the powerful emotions of
self-respect, family affection, and local loyalty. This does not

mean that we should stop speech training. But we shall not get near a common culture in Britain unless we make it a real social process – listening to ourselves and to others with no prior assumption of correctness – rather than the process of imitating a social class which is remote from most of us, leaving us stranded at the end with the 'two-language' problem. Nothing is more urgent than to get rid of this arbitrary association between general excellence and the habits of a limited social group. It is not only that there is much that is good elsewhere. It is also that, if you associate the idea of quality with the idea of class, you may find both rejected as people increasingly refuse to feel inferior on arbitrary social grounds.

Teaching writing

Here again we are faced with the problem of a necessary kind of training being limited by old ideas. It is not only that many of us are taught to write in old-fashioned styles. It is also that the forms we are taught often have little to do with the actual writing we need to practise.

In practice speaking, we are often limited to the formal debate or the casual three-minute speech, though neither, as taught, plays much real part in social life. We need to practise, therefore, such forms as the committee discussion, the verbal report, or the detailed questioning of a speech. Similarly, in writing, we need to practise not only the essay, but also the written report, the memorandum and minutes. One of the few common applied forms we now have is the business letter (perhaps not quite so terrible as it was, but still, as it comes through the post, pretty bad). We could do with regular practice in all kinds of correspondence – the letter of protest to the local paper as often as the acknowledgement of your 'kind favour'. We could also do with some practice in writing official forms, not only because so many are unnecessarily difficult, but also because their ordinary social tone is as regularly a kind of licensed bullying as that of the commercial letter is a kind of non-committal crawling. It would be something if we could learn to write to each other, on official or business occasions, in ways compatible with a self-respecting democratic society.

Teaching creative expression

Much of the best practice, in speech and writing, is and ought to be of a creative kind. In our junior schools, particularly, we have learned the value of making poems, stories, plays, figures, pictures, models, music, dance. Some of this work is excellent by any standards. Most of it is interesting. But the major limitation now built into this kind of teaching is that it is regarded as a form of *play*. This means that at a certain age it can be safely dropped, and put away with other childish things.

It is indeed play in the sense that most of us enjoy doing it. But these creative activities are also forms of work: for many adults, the work to which they give their whole lives. It is only the prejudice of a very narrow and early industrial society that the value of these activities is seen as a sort of harmless and indifferent play or therapy. From these activities comes much of man's real society, and they should be given that kind of respect throughout education. In the changes that come with puberty, it is vital that the practice of these activities should be continued, with no setting of 'more real' or 'more practical' work above them. Otherwise there is unnecessary fading, and all the major arts are relegated to the sphere of 'leisure': a separation which in itself makes inevitable, and much deeper than it ever now needs to be, a separation between art and society. Both sides then suffer: the arts because they are seen as marginal and specialized; society because it is limited to economics and administration.

It is depressing to think that much of this division is now actively taught and learned in our schools, which at an earlier stage do so much to show how important and satisfying the arts can be to almost everyone.

Teaching contemporary arts

The proper extension of creative practice is direct experience and discussion of all the contemporary arts at their best. The difficulty here is the common assumption that education has done its work when it has introduced us to a few classic authors. Of course we should get to know as much as we can of our inherited literature. But if we get to know it as a body of 'classics', we may sometimes confirm what is being taught elsewhere: that the arts are separate, in this case separate in time. It is significant how often, when culture is discussed, the idea of the museum is thrown in, often with real resentment.

In literature, to include contemporary work can have the good effect of unmaking the classics and remaking them as novels, poems, and plays. This is especially the case if living writers are invited into the educational process, at all possible stages, to read and talk about their work (as is now often possible through a scheme of the Regional Arts Associations). Even if we can only get records of people reading their own work, the atmosphere is still quite different. Similarly, we need not confine experience of painting to standard reproductions on the walls of schools and colleges. Many artists would be glad to be invited, and the local exhibition of painting or sculpture, or the building actually designed, discussed, and built in our own town, is always the place to start learning. Already, in music, composers have proved very willing to travel and play and discuss their work. This kind of contact, with creative artists and performers, is important above all because of the spirit it communicates.

We should be careful, moreover, not to play safe in these invitations: we should ask many kinds of creator and performer. The deepest danger, now, is the external division (pushed by the media, ratified by education) between those arts which are thought of as serious, academic, and old and those which are experienced as lively, personal, and new. To underwrite this division harms the traditional work and misses the chance of creating real standards in the new. In this respect, such forms as jazz and the cinema are crucial. Yet for one school performance and discussion of a good contemporary film there seem to be hundreds of visits to films of 'the classics' – versions of Dickens and Shakespeare made respectable by that fact, yet often inferior, as cinema, to new work. And then good new work is left mixed up in our minds with the bad work which our educational authorities think they are doing their duty by dismissing as inferior, negligible, and even dangerous. The resentment and confusion this causes has never been adequately appreciated. The only way to get some real movement and understanding is to bring in people who have actual standards, from their own work, and can communicate both its quality and its excitement.

Teaching the institutions

Because of the importance the institutions of communication now have in our society, we should include the teaching of certain basic facts about them in all our education. This should include something of their history and current social organization. It should include also some introduction to the ways in which they actually work.

The large impersonal media, such as the Press, the cinema, radio and television, come through to most people almost as acts of God. It is very difficult, without direct experience of their actual working, to see them as the products of men like

ourselves. I know that since I have seen something of television and radio production, and of publishing, I have quite
different attitudes to their finished work. It is a loss of naïvety
but also in many ways a gain in respect: more critical, in
every good sense, because more informed. If we are to feel
that our communication system belongs to the society,
instead of feeling that it is what 'they' have set up for us, this
kind of understanding of method must grow.

To follow through the real processes in producing a newspaper, a magazine, a book, a radio discussion programme, a
television play, a film, a dance, an opera, is usually exciting
and invariably educative. Much more of this can be done by
an intelligent use of modern resources. The only danger to
avoid is the quite common substitute for this work, in the
glamorized 'public relations' version of all these activities
which is now so often put out. If it is to be valuable, this kind
of teaching must base itself on the methods of education and
not of publicity, especially since all our cultural institutions
now suffer from the effects of this glamorized version, not
only on others but on the people working in the tension
between the glamour and the reality.

Teaching discussion

That education should be critical of all cultural work is often
the first point that springs to mind. Alertness is certainly
essential, but for a number of reasons we have interpreted
this so narrowly that there has been real damage. It is wholly
wrong, for example, if education is associated with 'criticism'
while the non-educational world is associated with practice.
Personal practice, direct experience of the arts, understanding of the institutions, should all come first. And response
should develop as an aspect of each of these kinds of teaching,
for it will always be limited, and sometimes even damaging,
if it is really separated from them. In teaching 'the classics'

we are usually not responsive enough. We substitute a dull and inert 'appreciation' which nobody can go on believing in for long. But then in teaching or commenting on all other work, we are usually so confident and so fierce that it is difficult to believe we are the same people. 'All that muck in the cinemas and on television' too often follows the routine remarks on the charm of the *Essays of Elia*, and neither does anybody any good.

Our real purpose should be to bring all cultural work within the same world of discourse: to see the connections between Elia and the manufactured television personality as well as the difference in value between *Lord Jim* and *Captain Condor*. We have to learn confidence in our own real opinions, and this depends on a kind of openness and flexibility, from the beginning, which much that is called 'criticism' does nothing to help. It will only ever be real education if the process by which judgements are arrived at is shared by all those who are expected to underwrite the judgements or take them over. We can be certain that some of the judgements will not be agreed. But that is all right, for as the argument continues we learn what real cultural discussion is.

Nearly all of us need help in seeing and judging the vast amount of work which comes our way. In education, we must be prepared to look at the bad work as well as the good. The principle in the past has been that once you know the good you can distinguish the bad. In fact this depends on how well you know the good, how well and personally you know why it is good, and how close the bad work is, in form, to anything you have learned to discuss.

I am sure that we are neglecting the world of ordinary communication to which all of us, after education, go home or go on. Yet this has crucial bearings on the whole social process which education is supposed to prepare us for. There are many ways of including this ordinary world. For example:

(i) Regular comparative reading of the range of national newspapers, with a look at headlines and with some detailed
comparison of particular stories.

(ii) Discussion of the range of comics, with a detailed look at
some kinds of story and drawing, and comparison with relevant stories in books and with stories and essays on similar
topics written by pupils. For example, stories about schools
in comics could be compared with one or two of the traditional school stories, with contemporary stories such as
Jim Starling, and with 'before and after' school stories by
pupils. As a guide to this, Orwell's essay on 'Boys' Weeklies'
might be read and discussed. Or the fairly common 'rebel'
stories in comics might be discussed in relation to *Huckleberry
Finn*.

(iii) Discussion of advertisements of a particular commodity,
alongside one of the *Which?* reports on the same commodity.
The commodity could then be used and pupils could write
their own reports on it.

(iv) Discussion of selected stories in women's and teenagers'
magazines. At a later stage these could be compared, in
terms of their implicit values, with the replies to those seeking
advice in the same magazines.

(v) A comparative study of 'social images' of particular kinds of
profession. For example, compare the version of 'the scien-
tist' or 'the professor' in comics, in science-fiction stories, and
in television programmes in which actual scientists appear.
Other professions offering relevant material are policemen
and detectives (over the whole range from comics and magazines to crime films and plays and documentaries), doctors
and nurses, teachers, artists. Varying images of the criminal
could also be compared, from a wide range of communications material. The social image of trade unionists could also
be looked at, with material from films, television plays, television and radio interviews, and comparative newspaper
reports on a particular dispute or strike.

(vi) Comparative visual studies of kinds of modern architecture
and design, of the results of town planning and unplanned

development, of 'before and after' appearance where an
area has been redeveloped.

(vii) Regular discussions of comparable television programmes.

(viii) Writing reviews of a current film, and then comparing them
with published reviews, with publicity material, and with
recordings of broadcast reviews.

I have done some work along these lines with adult and
young-worker groups. I have been very much struck by the
way in which, particularly with young workers, ideas for new
kinds of study have come from the groups, once the work has
been started. Any educational programme of this kind should
be sufficiently flexible to allow these new issues to be followed
up.

Two general points need emphasis. First, it is unreasonable
to ask teachers to do this often difficult work without offering
them training in it. The teaching of communications is now
sufficiently important to be a regular part of college work.
A good deal of scattered material and experiment is ready
to draw on, but needs co-ordination in relation to training.
Two kinds of body are urgently required: a Communications
Centre with a staff able to supply catalogues of existing
material and to collect and prepare new material, particularly in the expensive visual fields; and an Institute of
Communications Research, at university level, undertaking
long-range research and analysis (the Centre for Contemporary Cultural Studies at Birmingham is an excellent
pioneering example of such an Institute). As these bodies
come into existence, links with teachers and with colleges
can easily be arranged. Meanwhile, the supply of facilities
to teachers willing to undertake this work, and the support
necessary in its early stages, are the responsibility of local
education authorities, and it is good to see that some of these
authorities are willing to assume it.

Second, it is clear that the addition of this work to existing curricula raises many problems of time. But we have to ask ourselves, in view of the importance of modern communications in society, and of their sometimes oblique relation to education itself, not whether we can afford to give the time but whether we can afford not to give it. The work can be done at all stages of education, but it is perhaps particularly important in adolescence: in the leaving years especially, for it is then that the conflict between the values of school and the values of the adult world is most obvious. There is no need, however, for the work to be confined to schools. It should be a central part of liberal studies courses in technical colleges, and of apprentice courses. It should form a main part of informal work in the youth service, and it should be a normal subject – it is already increasing – in adult education. We should also remember that a lot of this work can be done through the large communications services themselves: both in general programmes and as part of the now expanding educational programmes. This is particularly important, not only because it can often be done so well in such services as television and radio (though parts of the work will always require the small class), but also because we misconceive the problem if we set education against the major communications systems. There is much in them to criticize, but there is also much to praise. There are many producers already anxious to do this kind of work, both as a part of direct education and because they know how much their own opportunities for doing valuable work depend on the development of an informed, unprejudiced, critical public. In the present very important stage of expansion, it is vital that the many responsible people in communications should work as closely as possible with the educational services, and that teachers and educational administrators (who have often been prejudiced about the newer communication forms, frequently with good if partial reasons) should make a real effort to reciprocate.

AMENDING THE INSTITUTIONS

We cannot leave everything to education and to the most responsible producers. Even if we are not yet ready for fundamental reforms in the institutions of communication, there are many possible amendments within existing social terms. Most people would agree that we want institutions which are both free and responsible. The balance between freedom and responsibility is always difficult to strike, but in many other parts of our social life, and already to a considerable extent in communications, we have agreed on measures to ensure this balance. The proposals now offered are within this tradition.

One clear way of ensuring a balance between freedom and responsibility is to make sure that as many people as possible are free to reply and criticize. Responsibility is then not only a thing we ask other people to maintain. It is what we ourselves exercise, by the right to reply, the right to criticize and compare, and the right to distribute alternatives. All these rights exist in our society, in a general way. Yet many of the institutions of communication are so large and powerful that they can become, in their way, separate empires. Individuals and organizations are free to criticize them, but such criticism can easily be isolated and set aside as unrepresentative or even irresponsible (in fact, for lack of information, it sometimes is irresponsible in the sense that it is wrong). The question is whether we can find ways of ensuring free and responsible comment and criticism, and of distributing the actual range of work.

The Press

The continuing economic crisis of the Press has provoked a number of suggestions for short-term change or immediate intervention. A Royal Commission was appointed in June 1974 and is still sitting. The fertility of suggestions has in fact been matched by an extraordinary barrenness at any political level, but the problems are so urgent that even the political parties will eventually have to face them. The conventional explanation of the crisis is that newspapers are overmanned, that unions are resistant to necessary technical changes, and that if these problems are overcome the industry can be 'slimmed' and 'made viable'. This is the familiar policy of capitalist rationalization, involving not only redundancies and unemployment, but the reduction of a varied service to a small number of relatively standard items. The political pressure to adopt such a solution will be intense, and must be intensely resisted. The problems of technical change are in fact inevitable, and it is true that in a general climate of competitive suspicion there has been a tendency in the unions to adopt defensive and conservative policies. New methods, conditions and levels of employment will undoubtedly come, in one form or another. But the press is not simply an industry to be rationalized, and its political range is already indefensibly narrow. It is in this wider context that forms of intervention have been sought: controls on the price of newsprint; a newsprint levy, with distribution of its proceeds to maintain a wide range of papers; selective levies on advertising, or on the proportions between advertising and editorial material; a small circulation bounty; government subsidies, as in Sweden, to maintain a just political representation; a national printing corporation. All these proposals deserve careful consideration. The time to introduce one or more of them must be in the very next case of a national newspaper being seriously threatened with closure. The Report of the Royal Commission, with its detailed analyses, may well come too late, and may well recommend the quite different policies of reduction and rationalization. The agency for such interventions should be in the first instance the working journalists and productive workers on the newspaper concerned, through their own organizations and through any emergency organization. This is crucial as a way of countering the inevitable propaganda against Government or State interference in the Press. The issue must be seen as it is: as a form of public protection of a necessary service, which is being given up in such an instance by its present owners, but which can be sustained and reorganized by the people who actually run it. If an immediate direct subsidy is necessary, while other measures are being devised and discussed, that will be the first step to take, and will deserve and require organized public support.

The Press Council

The Report of the 1947–9 Royal Commission on the Press recommended the creation of a Press Council, 'to consider where it [the Press] is going and consciously to foster those tendencies which make for integrity and for a sense of responsibility to the public'. It proposed a minimum of twenty-five members, of whom five, including the full-time chairman, should be lay members, eight representing proprietors, four editors, and eight other journalists. Two out of fifteen members of the Commission made reservations that the Press Council should not include lay members. When the Press Council was actually set up, this minority view prevailed and there were twenty-five members, of whom fifteen were editorial (eight elected by editors' organizations, seven by journalists' organizations), and ten managerial (elected by proprietors' organizations). In 1963, after a further Royal Commission, the Council was reconstituted, to include twenty per cent lay membership, and an independent chairman. The Council meets quarterly, in private, but its General Purposes Committee meets at least monthly. The Council issues special statements and an annual report. Anyone may refer a complaint against a newspaper to the Council, but it is not required to consider complaints by persons not directly concerned with the item, though in practice it has done so. A complaint is first referred to the editor concerned, and is sometimes settled at this stage. Otherwise, the Council considers it, at first through its General Purposes Committee. It invites witnesses, though it cannot compel their attendance, and issues reports and recommendations, though it cannot enforce these. Some editors have complied with recommendations; some have not.

Within its existing terms, the Press Council has done much good work. It has made many thorough investigations and reports on complaints, and has usefully reminded us that not every complaint against the Press is justified or even accurate. Yet in many fields it is quite without power or even influence (as in the closure of newspapers and magazines, which is one of the most serious current threats to a free Press), and even in its chosen field of specific complaints its authority can be questioned, in view of its composition. It has happened (Muggeridge case, 5th report, pp. 27–8) that an editor complained against has been a member of the Council considering the complaint. It is not stated what procedure is followed in such cases.

In 1961, I wrote that three reforms deserved urgent consideration.

(i) That the majority recommendation on the composition of the Press Council be adopted, thus providing for the inclusion of lay representatives and an independent chairman. The Royal Commission's argument that this would increase the Council's authority, and promote public confidence in it, seems still unanswerable. The degree of direct Press representation would still be such that there could be no question of the Press being controlled by some outside body. Yet the legitimate interests of the rest of society would in this way find some independent voice.

(ii) That while it is obviously wrong that any such Council should have authority over editors, the present position, in which even where a mis-statement of fact has been proved to the Council's satisfaction there is no obligation on editors to correct it, is very unsatisfactory. It cannot be seriously argued that the obligation to correct a publicly proved mis-statement of fact would be a threat to the freedom of the Press in any real sense, and it is clearly in the public interest that such mis-statements should be corrected. The legal position is difficult, but the Council might publicly invite the subscription of all proprietors and editors to this minimum obligation, and publish any such undertakings and refusals.

(iii) That since the major threat to the freedom of the Press is now the fact that newspapers and magazines can be closed down without warning, sometimes overnight, it should be enacted that any such proposal for closure be notified to the Press Council, which would have the duty of inquiring into all the relevant facts, hearing evidence from any persons concerned in the closure (particularly those whose livelihood is directly affected), and publishing its findings. The difficulties here are obvious, but it is even more difficult to take seriously those who say they value freedom of publication, yet claim exemption from timely public inquiry into cases where such freedom is suddenly denied.

Since 1961, some significant progress has been made, in just these fields. The Council, as now constituted, is a more evidently authoritative body, and many of its detailed reports are valuable. The Council has reported that it is now better known to the public, as a resource in cases of complaint. It is possible that, with this increasing authority, the Council will not need to follow the procedures suggested in (ii) above, but vigilance on this important matter is still necessary. The field of changes of ownership, and the problems of concentrated control, remain difficult. The 1962 Commission recommended a Press Amalgamation Court, but the Monopolies and Mergers Act (1965) indicated that questions affecting newspaper ownership and control would be dealt with by a specially appointed panel of the Monopolies Commission, and that this, rather than a court of law, should be the investigating body. The Press Council intends to report publicly on changes in ownership and control. If we are thinking of amending rather than changing so important an institution as the Press, it is probable that these lines of development are the right ones: publicity and the machinery of public inquiry are important factors in so public a field. Yet the economic pressures are so great that there is a tendency to leave the matter at the level of report and disquiet. More substantial changes will become inevitable.

Government Advertising

It is necessary to look at one crucial matter, where Government policy has already a direct influence. The amount of money spent on advertising by Government departments and public undertakings is already a significant factor in press revenue and it is being regularly increased. Some of this advertising is objectionable in itself (see especially the military recruiting campaigns, with their shocking imagery of adventure, and the competing fuel and power campaigns, which make no social or economic sense). But some is useful or marginal (post office, road safety, etc.). At present, the distribution of this advertising, paid for by public money, follows the ordinary commercial patterns, and a newspaper like the *Morning Star*, for example, justifiably complained of its exclusion. In the eighteenth and early nineteenth centuries, Government advertising was selectively used, for political reasons. Today, the selective pattern is primarily commercial, though given the present social structure of the

Press it is not without political effect. I believe it is time for a public inquiry into the whole field of Government and public authority advertising, and it would be useful to raise at this inquiry the question of the role of this public money in the present economic structure of the Press. A reforming government might well consider whether this flow of public money

Government Press Advertising		Government Press Advertising	
£ Expenditure, 1965–6		£ Expenditure, 1965–6	
Express	314,892	Times	54,993
Mail	125,602	News of the World	142,007
Mirror	381,485	Observer	104,798
Sketch	20,933	People	182,231
Telegraph	200,247	S. Citizen	3,590
Financial Times	29,511	S. Express	199,322
Guardian	36,605	S. Mirror	86,715
Morning Star	—	S. Times	198,589
Sun	43,973		

(Source: Financial Secretary to the Treasury, 1967)

ought, as a matter of social policy, to be directed in such ways that it counteracts the present alarming development of concentrated Press ownership and control. The whole matter is evidently contentious, but the argument should now take place, and in public.

Books and magazines

For the first time ever in Britain, we have become used, since the war, to a range of good cheap books. This was one of the most important things that has ever happened in our cultural history: that books of a kind which, in previous periods would have reached only a very small public, could be easily and cheaply distributed, and in fact find a much larger public. All our old assumptions about a tiny minority of serious readers have had, in practice, to be revised.

Yet the spread of paperbacks, and of cheap educational books of all kinds, has created new problems. A new kind of owner has come into publishing, attracted by the new possibility of large profits. The scale of capital involved is rising, and as a direct result there are constant amalgamations of publishers, and the disappearance of many independent houses. Already many of the apparently independent names of publishers, on book jackets, are simply the trading names of different parts of large publishing organizations. This powerful movement towards concentration of ownership is a severe threat to the freedom and diversity of writing. It is not only that fewer people are deciding what ought to be published. It is also that, to succeed in an increasingly competitive market, there is a new and sometimes desperate emphasis on a reasonably certain and very rapid sale. The best publishers are under constant pressure from the competition of the worst, and they get very little public help.

We need to maintain a wide range of independent publishers, and the critical moment is now. As a first step, we need a Books Council, representative of publishers, booksellers, and authors. This Council would collect and publish the existing facts, and would report on all major changes. It would also review existing distribution arrangements, which are near the heart of the matter.

Most towns in Britain are without an adequate independent bookshop. The distribution of books and magazines, outside a few fortunate centres, is in the hands of powerful chains of shops. These chains apply to books and magazines simple tests of quantity. Below a certain likely selling figure, they are not interested, and will not even offer the item for sale. (They are said also to refuse certain publications, on 'moral' grounds. These are not exactly apparent, when one looks at the familiar counters.) Thus the successful book or magazine will get around, but the book or magazine which might be bought, if it were available on anything like equal terms, will in many cases simply not be there. Even in paperbacks, where there is quite good distribution of the full range, there is increasing pressure towards the book that will sell quickly, so that there is no problem of holding stocks. If this situation is allowed to persist and develop, the real opportunities of the coming of cheap books will be missed.

An important part of all new work, in literature and opinion, appears at first in the independent reviews or 'little magazines'. We have a good range of such magazines, of all kinds, but they have little chance with the chain shops. We simply do not know, until we have tried, what public these magazines might actually reach. And the people who say whether we can try or not are the owners of the chain shops.

There is need for a Books Council, simply to publish and review the facts. But I would like to see it go further. It should have the power, and the necessary capital grant, to set up real bookshops in the hundreds of places now served only by the chains. The Council would know, as anyone who uses books and magazines at all closely would know, the difference between a real bookshop and the ordinary chain-shop branch. If it found that in any sizeable community there was no real bookshop, it could either establish its own, or help the public library to establish a bookshop as an ancillary to its lending service, an extension which the development of the reading public now makes reasonable. The chain shops would of course fight this, and might even, in the process, mend their own policies. But if we value the free availability of books and magazines, we should not be afraid of that kind of opposition. The alternative, under existing economic pressures, is an increasingly rigid and mechanical system, under which large publishing organizations feed certain quick-selling items to large distributing organizations, with every kind of minority work restricted to small independent channels. I do not see how anybody who thinks of books as more than simple commodities can stay silent or inactive in the face of that kind of development. But it is not only a matter of expressing opposition. We need an alternative organization, of a positive kind, to unite the many publishers, booksellers, and authors who are already aware of the dangers, and who see the opportunities of the present expansion if it is not allowed to be abused.

We need also to note the paradoxical effects on writers of these changes, and of the general expansion in books. The economics of writing has reached a point of absurdity, in that almost any ancillary activity – teaching, reviewing, lecturing, editing, broadcasting – is, by comparison with the writing of almost all books, so much better paid that a cynic might suppose people only write books to gain access to these more rewarded activities. A few carefully publicized financial successes mask a general situation in which, for most people, writing is a form of sweated labour. Moreover an unpleasant kind of cynicism has grown up around this: writers are so vain, and so many people want to be writers, that the sweated labour doesn't matter: you couldn't stop them doing it if you tried. Of course part of this is true; the ambition to write is widespread and the need to write is quite common. But there are too many people living comfortably off the writing of others, or constantly using what living writers have produced, to make what is at first an easy joke in any way tolerable. There are several things that can be done. First an effective amendment of copyright law is necessary to deal with the widespread use, in education, of the work of living writers, without permission and without fee. It is important that modern writing is studied in schools and universities, but it is now often photocopied and distributed, in what amount to massive numbers, without any return to its originators.

have heard a young university lecturer, on a secure and ample pensioned salary, express indignation at the idea of paying a fee to a young poet, with no such advantages, whose work he had copied and was teaching. A system of licensing, with payment, of educational institutions is now being discussed and should be quickly put into operation. It is often supposed that writers will be so flattered that their work is being discussed that they will take unauthorized photocopying as a compliment which puts payment out of the question. The convenience of this supposition is sustained by the fact that the writers concerned are virtually never asked which, in practice, they would prefer.

Secondly, the campaign for Public Lending Right deserves early success. It is ironic that the excellence of the British public library system, sustaining high levels of book-reading by comparison with most similar societies, has led, not unnaturally, to comparatively low levels of actual book-buying. The campaign led by the Writers' Action Group has asked for a change in the law which would entitle writers to a fee, paid from central funds and not directly by borrowers, when one of their books is borrowed from a library. An alternative scheme, based on payment when a book is purchased by a library, is opposed by most writers, mainly because in the form in which it has been presented it would exclude all books already in libraries, which would be radically unfair to writers who have already done most of their work, and might be expressed as a percentage of selling price, which would be unfair because there is no consistent relationship between the price of a book and the amount of time and work put into it. The lending fee scheme, based on modern data sampling techniques, has been shown to be practical, and is already in operation elsewhere. Both major political parties have supported a Lending Right legislation, and a Bill was announced in the Queen's Speech of 1974. At the time of writing it is still awaited, and the whole question has been surrounded by a process of evasion and double-talk which it is hoped will be eventually recorded. The sustained and generous enactment of this right is indeed urgently necessary.

Thirdly, there needs to be some discussion of a tendency which is related to changes in publishing organization and techniques: one which can be summarized as a crucial change in the way in which most books originate. Many people still have the model of a writer getting an idea for a book, writing it, and then offering it to a publisher. In a number of cases this older pattern still holds. But an increasing number of books are conceived within publishing organizations as 'slots' in a series, or as books 'needing to be written' or, more commonly, 'for which there would be an obvious sale'. Writers are then sought out and commissioned. In a number of cases it is a perfectly satisfactory procedure, but as it becomes dominant it carries certain obvious dangers. Such books, it is said, are easier to sell. The publishers already know (or think they know, which is just as common) which kinds of books are wanted. A production and distribution system organized around such books may then find little room for the kind of book which is still, among writers and readers, taken as normal – the book which someone positively wanted to write. In the difficult economic situation of writers, the offer to write some other book is obviously relatively difficult to refuse. Not many people are asked to sell their souls; no more, perhaps, than go around offering to sell them. But there is a range of marginal choices, between the book which could be done, for which an advance is available, and for which (it is said) the demand already exists, and the other book which, without such prompting, might actually be written, only to stay in the drawer. It is difficult to gather all the evidence. People defend their choices after they have been made. The books not written, or indefinitely delayed, while these more pressing opportunities were accepted, can not of course speak for themselves. Yet it is my firm impression that there has been a significant change in the origination of books and then in their character and quality. To the extent that this depends upon alterable tendencies in publishing, now based increasingly on the market-survey and the speed-and-volume calculations developed in other large-scale capitalist production, there is a point of common interest, among writers and I believe among readers, which has to be defined, defended and developed.

Advertising

There has been widespread concern, in recent years, about alleged abuses in advertising. In the past, certain safeguards have been codified, notably in relation to the advertising of 'cures' for certain major diseases. Yet a substantial amount of public anxiety remains, and there is a continual but dispersed controversy, between advertising practitioners and their critics, over the facts and values in question.

In 1961 I proposed an Advertising Council, an independent public body, to replace the existing Advertising Safeguards Authority, which makes and administers its own internal rules. This may still be necessary, though recent legislation on trade descriptions and the currently vigorous policy of the Office of Fair Trading are alternative ways of dealing with some of the more obvious problems. Consumer protection, as it is usually called, is in fact urgently necessary, after all the formal safeguards have apparently been satisfied.

For the rest I now believe that advertising cannot be tackled as an isolated issue, and that 'consumer protection', though so important in its own field, is only a limited response to the problem. The fact is that organized advertising now so permeates the whole communications system, and that its methods have been so widely extended into public relations and politics (where the overlap between market surveys and public opinion polling is especially significant), that beyond a vigorous consumer protection policy there are few intermediate measures; a whole social and economic system is quickly and radically challenged if anything more than local defensive measures is proposed. The only possible area of short-term change is in taxation policy; probably not by a general tax, which would be simply absorbed and passed on in prices, but by selective and variable levels of taxation related to the general economic management of demand. Much of the most relentless advertising is in fields where need and demand are marginal, or where there is an actual contradiction between the priorities of productive investment and this more immediately profitable investment. In the years of supposed boom this was more easily tolerated than it is likely to be in the coming years of relative scarcity. Left to itself, advertising will push harder in the very areas in which an agreed national policy would indicate quite different priorities in production and investment. It will be a test of the seriousness of any national production policy, whether the necessary intervention against this irresponsible social force (some of it now, significantly, controlled by interests quite outside this society) is firmly made, by selective taxation and other comparable measures.

Broadcasting and television

The Pilkington Report, published in 1962, marked a major advance in public discussion and awareness of the problems of broadcasting and television policy. The Report was heavily attacked by most of the Press, and there was an evident political nervousness about some of its main recommendations. It remains, however, an important point of reference for all reform in this field. In particular, its proposal for a further separation of programme provision from advertising, by making I.T.A. rather than the programme companies the advertising contractor, would still be a sensible first step. Its definitions of a responsible public policy are still the best criteria for judging the performance of the two authorities. In the years since it was published, two main developments can be noted. First, it is clear that the existence of commercial television has radically affected the B.B.C.'s attitude to its own services. As could easily have been predicted, the existence of the commercial emphasis, in so central a position, affects the whole field. The B.B.C., if it is to be responsible, can neither withdraw into a minority position, as most commercial interests would significantly like it to do, nor engage, as it is now increasingly doing, in a competition for audiences on the terms set by the commercial channel. Yet it is bound to follow one or other of these courses, while a major television service designed on the basis of profit rather than use remains in existence. Some signs of more responsible supervision by the I.B.A., in terms of its original function, and of certain changes of emphasis in the programme companies themselves, can certainly be welcomed, and may indeed be traced to the context of the Pilkington Report and to increased public interest in the process of the renewal of contracts. But it is now more than ever certain that we shall have to get rid of a commercial television structure, and especially of this one, with its close connections in ownership with our already con-centrated commercial press. The way forward is the creation of genuinely independent programme companies, which will be leased all necessary production and transmission facilities by an independent public authority. It was perhaps welcome that the B.B.C. got its second channel, but the concentration of control there is also disquieting. If the possible fourth channel is allotted, in a spurious balance, to the existing commercial interests, or to any similar grouping, we shall have lost for a generation any chance of making a genuinely public system.

But the alternative is not a limitless extension of the B.B.C. As each new service comes into technical availability, new forms of organization should be created. We could have, within our existing thinking, two or three independent public corporations, preferably regionally dispersed. In these ways, it would be possible to start dismantling both the present commercial structure of I.T.V. and the present centralization of the B.B.C., replacing them by a number of public corporations holding production and transmission facilities in trust (with the necessary minimum arrangements for technical coordination), and by a wider range of leasing programme companies, which would be responsible for production policy. Proposals of this general kind have been put to the current Annan Committee on Broadcasting.

The second fact to be noted, in the years since the Pilkington Report, is the growth of various pressure groups, with an aspiration to affect policy and content. This whole field of representation of the interests of listeners and viewers is extremely difficult. Some years ago it was proposed, notably by the Council for Children's Welfare in its report *Family Viewing*, that there should be a 'Viewers' Council . . . entirely independent of the television authorities and companies . . . a statutory body, not unlike the committee proposed by Sir William Beveridge in his 1949 Report on Broadcasting'. It has also been proposed by the Sound Broadcasting Society that the Council should be enlarged to become a Listeners' and Viewers' Council, and there has been discussion of associating this with the existing Radio and Television Safeguards Committee, which is 'a federation of all the sixteen trade-union and professional bodies operating in the field of radio and television; it covers everybody – actors, technicians . . . and so on'.

These proposals are useful, but everything will depend on the status of any such body. A number of advisory bodies already exist, but it is alleged that they are only rarely consulted on matters of substance. The question is whether it is better to have a completely independent body (with statutory obligation to report), or to work for a Broadcasting and Television Council, similar to those proposed for the Press and for advertising, on which the authorities as well as independent people would be represented. There seem to be clear advantages in the latter, provided there is regular public reporting. It was disquieting to see the brusque rejection, by B.B.C. and I.T.A., of the recommendations of the O'Conor Committee on Children and Television Programmes, even where the authorities had themselves set up the committee. A separate monitoring organization would be useful, but a Council in which all issues would have to be publicly argued and reported on is likely to be more in keeping with real public responsibility. It seems to be a fundamental failing of our society that we are continually directed towards a pattern in which on the one hand there are 'the authorities', and on the other hand there are the institutions of opposition and criticism. Each side, we are told, has its part to play. The reality of this usually comes through as an invitation to critics to speak their mind, but then, very often, they are simply brushed off, because 'the authorities', after all, have the final responsibility. I think we shall only get responsible institutions when policies have to be justified in open, equal, and regular discussion, which has a real chance of making some change. A Broadcasting and Television Council might achieve this. A Listeners' and Viewers' Council, while undoubtedly useful, would be important mainly as a step towards a broader sharing of responsibility.

Our continuing difficulty, in finding any open and public solution in this matter, is of course a main reason for the development of the various freelance pressure groups already referred to. I dislike the views of one or two of these groups, but I would insist that arrangements for public criticism and discussion are necessary. Certainly we can all ask who the pressure groups speak for, whether they are really 'the decent people of Britain' or whatever. But we can only ask this question in good faith if we are prepared to envisage genuine facilities for public comment and question. We shall have to see how things go, in the present competition between pressure groups, but it is probable, in my view, that we shall have to come back to the idea of a Broadcasting and Television Council, similar in scope and method to the reformed Press Council, if we are to achieve any settled public balance between freedom and responsibility, and prevent any further development of censorship by authority or demagogy. In fact it would be possible to combine some of the solutions to the problems of organization and of public representation by instituting a Broadcasting Council, which would represent and supervise the new public corporations and the principles of their relations with programme companies, and which would at the same time be a public forum for arguments about specific policies and programmes. A proposal for such a Council has been made to the Annan Committee, together with the useful additional proposal that there should be a properly funded Public Institute of Communications, taking over the functions of present internal 'audience research' and initiating more general research programmes on communications policies and their effects.

General

Any public body can become ingrown or even corrupt, and public responsibility is never fully discharged by the setting up of organizations, however sensibly these are composed. The need for open public discussion and criticism, outside organizations, is absolute. In many ways the conditions for this exist, but there are some important uncertainties. We say we have freedom of comment, within the law, but in practice this is not always how it actually feels. For example, it seems that almost anything can be said about a book or a play or a politician, but that it is dangerous to say the same kind of thing about a soap or a stove or a fountain-pen. It is sometimes said, by editors, that the existing freedom of comment on books and plays depends, legally, on actual invitations to comment on them by sending copies or tickets for review. Whether this is really so in law I am not in a position to say; I have heard it authoritatively doubted. But the effect in practice seems to be of this kind, and I do not think anyone could say that commercial organizations have to face the kind of specific public criticism of their products which is regularly faced by authors and publishers, producers and actors, composers and performers, painters, athletes, politicians, and scholars. The excellent work of the consumers' advisory bodies, in such publications as *Which?*, which used to be confined to the membership of a particular association, is now often reported in the press and in broadcasting, yet the law in this field still creates many difficulties and uncertainties, and many people learn a practical prudence in this kind of comment. It is right, of course, that we should all be protected from defamation, but the public interest now seems very unevenly defined. The specific review of products and services should be as commonplace in our newspapers and broadcasting and television as the reviewing of books and plays. I wrote in 1961: 'to televise *Which?* would be an invaluable service, and might properly be the B.B.C.'s answer to the commercials of I.T.V.'. This is now often done in different kinds of programmes, and has been popular and effective. Some manufacturers argue that they ought not to be exposed to public reports and criticism which may very well, in some cases, turn out to be wrong. What they then have to show, however, is why they should be a special case. So long as there is always the right to reply, open public comment is central to a good society, and it is time to start applying it over the whole range, getting rid of the remaining protected areas. It would be useful if the law in these matters could be publicly reviewed and clarified, so that we all really know where we stand. Any necessary changes might then also be clarified and worked for.

CHANGING THE INSTITUTIONS

A great deal of good can undoubtedly be done by extending our education in communications and by amending or developing existing institutions. It is certain that this is the work to which we should go as a matter of urgency. Yet it is clear to me that beyond this immediate range certain other actions are necessary. The great majority of those I have called the contributors are employed by groups which have no real responsibility, either to the society or to the cultural purposes they ought to serve. The main feature of such groups is that they provide the capital with which the service can be operated. The society then gets what they decide to offer, and the actual producers are encouraged to compete in supplying it. This seems to me intolerable, in a society wishing to describe itself as free. Yet we are deeply confused in thinking about possible alternatives: partly by the propaganda of the existing groups, who insist very loudly that freedom for them is freedom for everybody; and partly by the genuine difficulties of any public cultural system. We have been reduced to making contrasts between the speculator and the bureaucrat, and wondering which is the blacker devil. The real barrier, perhaps, is that we see these as the only alternatives.

The dangers of State control are real, especially in centralized modern communications. Moreover, our commercial culture emerged by fighting State control, of an earlier kind, and has active memories of its dangers. Against this, many socialists point out that we now have control of another kind, and that it is becoming increasingly centralized. This is true, but until we can show a convincing alternative, which is free of these dangers, it is no kind of reason to change.

I believe that the principle of such an alternative can be stated, and that its practice can be learned. It is this. Where the means of communication can be personally owned, it is the duty of society to guarantee this ownership and to ensure that distribution facilities are adequate, on terms compatible with the original freedom. Where the means of communication cannot be personally owned, because of their expense and size, it is the duty of society to hold these means in trust for the actual contributors, who for all practical purposes will control their use.

Personal ownership is possible in the work of most individual artists. I think much more should be done to provide facilities for such artists, where they are wanted. Local authorities could build studios to let to painters, and bursaries could be offered to young writers and musicians, to go on with their work, just as bursaries are now offered in formal education and scholarship. A good deal of work could be offered to artists, by local education authorities, in the teaching or showing of contemporary arts as described above – particularly, of course, showing (taking this to include readings and performances as well as exhibitions in the visual arts). Artists often teach best by simply showing their work, rather than having to talk about it. Existing experiments such as giving membership of an educational institution to artists, simply to have them there, could be very widely extended. In distribution, there could be many more publicly supported exhibitions and performances, of a local kind. If any artist did not want to use these facilities, he would have the same freedom as now. But we should not assume in advance that all artists prefer to be left alone, when this is understood as left alone to fight through the market, with the constant implication that they would have been all right if they had taken up some 'real' or 'socially useful' job. I am sure that even the most generous offering of facilities of this kind would be met by an even more generous response, from artists glad to show their work and glad to think there are people even potentially interested in it. If funds are needed for these facilities, beyond the ordinary public revenue on which they are already an authorized charge, it would be worth looking at the whole question of the money now made from artists of the past. A ten-year extension of copyright, for example, might be reasonably made the basis of a new trust fund, to be administered by authors' and musicians' professional organizations to help young writers and composers. In the sale of paintings, where large sums of money are now made by speculators and dealers, a compulsory percentage contribution to a similar trust fund could be devised. Such measures would have the advantage of reminding us of the real situation: that while in any one generation artists may need help, and if they get it may find it described as subsidy or charity, in fact, in the history of a people, artists create not only spiritual but material wealth. When this can no longer go to the artists and their immediate families, there is surely no better way of using it than to help their successors, as a matter of right. It is very important to put the question in this way. Everyone seems to ask 'who will pay for the arts?', but what needs to be said – even harshly against some of the ordinary patronage and philistinism – is that the arts pay for themselves, and more than pay. The only real problems are administrative: how to arrange what is in effect the necessary credit, and how to ensure that the values represented by established art are made available to art itself, rather than to private profit or state display.

The proposal for an extension of copyright was listed for consideration in the 1965 White Paper 'A Policy for the Arts'. It is now again being considered by the Whitford Committee. In an open letter, *A Policy for the Writer*, the Society of Young Publishers supported the idea, and proposed that the period of extension should be twenty-five rather than ten years. The Society went further and proposed that after the present fifty years, permanent copyright should be vested in the State, to provide money for helping authors. This proposal has been usefully linked with the funding of Public Lending Right, and is indeed relevant to it, though the funding of Public Lending Right is really a responsibility already incurred to authors by the public funding of the Library Service. Meanwhile we should remember a further proposal of the Society, that we should inquire into the idea of a State publishing house, on the lines of an independent public corporation, with special policies in the reissue of classics and in new non-commercial work. These two ideas – of copyright extension, and a National Publishing House – might eventually be combined, but meanwhile we can work for each on its merits.

At a certain point we touch the edges of that huge cultural organization which is at once the most difficult and the most necessary to reform. In television, in cinemas, in theatres, and in the Press we find a scale of investment beyond the possibility of ownership by individual contributors, and a degree of profit so large as to make any attempt to assert the public interest a fight from the start. I see no alternative, in these fields, but public ownership. The millions of pounds involved could come from no other source. Yet there would be no point in this change if for contributors it was merely the substitution of one form of external control for another. We have to try to combine, in a proper balance, the reasonable provision of public money and the direct freedom of contributors.

We have, fortunately, a precedent, described by Lord Ashby as

a most ingenious British social invention for . . . supervising public expenditure on science and scholarship; the invention of appointing controllers who are drawn from the ranks of the controlled: scientists to administer grants for scientific research, medical men to administer grants for medical research, and academic men to administer grants to universities. It is assumed, and the assumption has been abundantly justified, that controllers of this calibre can determine, better than politicians or administrators can, the criteria for exercising control.

It is true that science and scholarship are different from general communications. But their importance is no greater, to a civilized democratic community. The only alternative to control by a few irresponsible men, who treat our cultural means as simple commodities, is a public system. There will always be tension, in any such system, but the precedent of the universities, which could not survive without public money yet which have retained their academic freedom while accepting it, is important. Theoretically, the State could now dictate to the universities, under the threat of withholding funds. In practice there can be no such dictation, though there can be tension and argument, which in fact are useful. Academic freedom is at least as vulnerable as the general freedom of cultural contribution, yet it has not been killed or weakened by the public system we have. An important element in this, undoubtedly, is that the universities, as bodies, are the organized scholars and teachers to whom this freedom is necessary, and who can defend the principle in a collective way.

Any public ownership of the means of communication should include, as an integral part of its system, the creation of independent professional companies. The outlines of these exist, and much of our best work already comes from companies which can pursue long-term independent policies, creating styles and traditions of their own. Individual journalists, actors, film directors, and producers have usually now to submit to hiring by the financial interests which have real control. Under the new system proposed, the means of communication would be publicly owned but vested in independent trusts which would include representatives of the professions concerned. Use of the media would then be allotted by long-term contract to independent professional companies, which would have full control over content and policy.

In the theatre, for example, more theatres could be nationally owned, and others owned by municipalities. In either case a particular theatre (or, to meet real production needs, a group of two or three theatres) would be leased to a company of actors, producers, and dramatists. The main duty of the public trust concerned would be to ensure that the company was adequately organized for the general work it proposed to do, and to see that the range of companies was representative of all trends and schools. Meanwhile it is worth recording that there has been, in the past few years, a marked change of mood, among some local authorities, on this kind of public provision. The best authorities, planning and building theatres and arts centres, are already a model for a generation ahead.

In the cinema, film production facilities could similarly be made available to companies of professional film-makers. The cinema circuits could be publicly owned, in two or three networks, and a grant of production facilities would guarantee distribution on one of these. The present concentration of distribution facilities has been wholly stultifying. An immediate start should be made on one public circuit, linked to a reconversion of some production facilities to an independent public company. As things now are, film-makers are in the hands of financial controllers who decide whether a film is worth making before it can be made. As Karel Reisz put it, film makers have to choose subjects 'acceptable to the system', 'not working on the best possible subjects that you want to treat but on the best subjects possible'. In a sensible public system, these decisions would be in the hands of the film-makers themselves, both through the representative public trust and by the giving of contracts for facilities not on the basis of one film but to a professional company aiming to develop its work over several years.

In television, there could be a similar system. The means of production and transmission could be publicly owned but vested in several independent trusts, to include representatives of the actual providers of programmes. The facilities could then be leased, over a period, to professional companies or groups of companies, who would decide their own work. There could be liaison, here, between the professional television companies and the film and theatre companies; also with orchestras and bands, and with the existing guilds of individual contributors.

The b.b.c. has an excellent definition of 'public-service broadcasting', but it exemplifies the dangers of a very large organization, in which producers can become subject to administrators. The development of regional and local broadcasting could become the means of transferring control of this public-service broadcasting to the producers themselves, who already have the nucleus of independent regionally based companies. Here, as in all the proposed companies, it is vital that we should break the pattern of the actual producer controlled by the administrator. There is no reason why all such companies should not be run by ordinary democratic means, with all members having an equal say in discussion of policy, and with administrators working within the definitions of an elected policy, like all other members.

The huge concentration of power in the Press will take a long time to remedy. The first step should be to free local newspapers from remote control by financial empires. A Local Newspapers Trust, in which working editors and journalists would have a majority, could be publicly financed to regain ownership. Local trusts could be organized, to guarantee the independence of editors, with a right of appeal to the national body. A reformed Press Council, retaining a majority of journalists, could then examine the more difficult fields of national newspapers and magazines. The aim should be, as elsewhere, to hold the production facilities in trust, through public ownership where necessary, for allocation to companies of working journalists who would decide their own policies. The functionless financial groups which now control most of our newspapers could be steadily cut out, and the Press restored to the only people capable of guaranteeing its freedom: the working journalists themselves. Meanwhile, the newsprint companies should be taken into separate public ownership. Here is a raw material which should not be tied to particular newspaper proprietors and combines, but should be available, at a fair and open price, to all who wish to use it.

On advertising, there is a continuing case for particular measures of public safety, along the lines already devised for patent medicines, and there is also a strong case for reducing the amount of advertising expenditure that is now allowed to be set off against tax, and for some selective direct taxation. But a more positive answer is very much needed. We need information and advice on the wide range of goods now available, but advertising is a very primitive way of supplying it. A great deal of information about our needs and preferences is now locked up in the offices of advertising agents, who use it only as it suits them, to help them sell a particular product. It is important that this information should be made generally available, if necessary by new independent research, and used in the general public interest as a guide to social and economic policy. The right way to give specific information and advice is that pioneered by the consumers' advice organizations. These should be freed of present legal restrictions, and encouraged, as independent bodies helped by public grant, to extend their work beyond distribution of the kind of printed report which inevitably reaches only a minority. It would be possible to establish actual centres, in the main shopping areas, with the results of tests visually demonstrated, with free advice made available, and with travelling displays and comparative exhibitions of quality and design. Many of the best skills now used in advertising and selling could be used unambiguously for the public good, in such a service. The idea of such centres, first suggested some fifteen years ago, has recently been taken up and put into practice, on a small but growing scale. It has been especially linked to problems of comparing and monitoring prices, and this is important. But this is not the only or even the main advantage of such centres, which should be primarily sources of independent public information on goods and services, deliberately overriding all special interests.

The communication of real information, and the continual challenge to make judgements of quality, can make a radical difference to our whole economic life, in a proper combination of freedom and responsibility. For it is wrong to set affluence against quality. A central problem of our society is to bring them together, in the common interest. The gimmicks and false appeals which have given affluence a bad name must be challenged in the interests of real use, good design, and a sense of proportion about commodities. Much of the future of our society depends on the growth of real values in this dynamic field. This growth will come about only if we can all take part in it in the course of ordinary living.

CONCLUSION

Many of the measures proposed are radical. All need further definition. But already, at the level of theory, we have broken the deadlock which is so obviously damaging our society. We can conceive a cultural organization in which there could be genuine freedom and variety, protected alike from the bureaucrat and the speculator. Actual work would be in the hands of those who in any case have to do it, and the society as a whole would take on the responsibility of maintaining this freedom, since the freedom of individual contribution is in fact a general interest. At the same time, we would have broken out of the social situation in which it is taken for granted that the arts and learning are minority interests, and that the ordinary use of general communications is to get power or profit from the combination of people's needs and their inexperience. We would be using our means of communication for their most general human purposes.

That is one way of development, but of course it will be opposed. The link with advertising, observed again and again in our study of institutions and methods, is not accidental or marginal. It is the reflection of a capitalist society in which commercial interests claim priority in every area of life, and we have had this emphasis and its practical results just long enough to persuade many of us that it is a natural order. The only other effective version of communications in the world is a plain association with the winning or maintenance of political power. Against these versions, with their great institutions absorbing a majority of talent in every generation, we cannot expect any easy struggle. The fact that change will in any case be difficult, that we shall run into many kinds of genuine difficulty and complication, will be tirelessly used to discourage us. There will always be voices, of many kinds, advising us to give up. But in the worst moments, now and in the future, I think we have only to look at the existing situation, clearly and honestly, to recover our energy. The systems have profited so far by each terrifying us with the other, and by the lack of any genuine and attractive alternative. I believe that under pressure the alternative is now emerging, in many minds, and with it a new kind of determination. Any useful change will have to be a genuine discipline, with a real sense of responsibility and with as many people as possible taking part. I think there is a good chance of this happening, but it is only a chance and will need all our strength. At least, now, the challenge is clear.

RETROSPECT AND PROSPECT, 1975

THIS book was conceived in 1960, in what seems, in retrospect, a very different Britain. Yet the first thing that struck me, working through it again, was the essential continuity of the crisis in communications. It is no kind of satisfaction to see that the analysis of the condition of the press, of tendencies in broadcasting and publishing, and of the subordination of a general communications process to an increasingly powerful system of advertising and public relations, has been strikingly confirmed. Since the analysis was first made, seven more national newspapers have been closed down, and as I write the future of several others is in serious doubt. Commercial interests, having made their way into television, have gained a foothold – fortunately still precarious – in sound broadcasting, and are keeping up their pressure to exploit such new developments as cable. Book publishing has moved much further into a combine phase, and the working conditions of authors have sharply deteriorated. All these and similar tendencies of the period as a whole have been critically exposed by the current economic crisis, but this is not their cause. On the contrary, the system first identified in 1960 is genuinely structural. General recession brings it more clearly into view, but the crisis is not external to the system; it is part of it.

It is now all the more necessary to say this because the people who developed and operated the system, and who are still in control of it, are quick, by the nature of their trade, to find short-term explanations of their own difficulties and of the serious difficulties in which they have involved others. In a local sense, which must not be taken as flattering, they are indeed masters of displacement. It is clear, looking back, that the period from the late fifties to the early seventies in Britain was a time of evasion of all the structural problems of the society. But this was not, as it is now at times represented, the result of general inattention. The evasion was systematic, and the communications institutions were one of its central agencies. From about 1958 until the economic crisis of the winter of 1973–74 a social and cultural phase, articulated if not led by the media, deflected attention from all the long-run structural problems of the society, and offered a lively series of short-term definitions and interests. The celebration of the 'affluent' society, and of happy consumption, looks sick enough now, from a time of deep economic crisis and a million and a half unemployed. But it was always sick, beyond its lively cosmetic effects. When I described commercial advertising, in 1960, as 'the magic system' – the organized deflection of need and reason, by the organized propagation of false images of need and satisfaction – I had seen the beginning of the problem. What I then feared but did not expect was the persistence of this system beyond one danger-point after another, until when we all began to wake up, among the debris of the broken illusions, it was still there, and still offering, if with some changes of style, to promote a solution of the crisis which, it said confidently, other people had caused. When I first wrote this book I was looking forward to a Labour Government which I hoped would undertake at least some of the intermediate measures of reform. In 1966, with a Labour Government in power, I welcomed some of their proposals and could reasonably sustain this constructive perspective. It is now not only that we have to acknowledge that most of the serious proposals were contemptuously pushed aside, though it is true that they were revived and developed during a period of opposition in the early seventies, only to be pushed aside again on a return to power. It is also that in the depth of the present crisis we have to watch a Labour Government retaining the advertising and public relations industry as an agency in tackling the crises of energy-shortage and inflation. The most plausible formation for intermediate reform has thus, in this period, not only defaulted on its own best purposes but at the level of government has shown itself, unmistakably, to be an active part of the very system which it has appeared to oppose. In this sense, the period of this book shows a movement from a time of warning but also of hope to a time which could easily be interpreted as one of despair.

But then the original analysis was an analysis of contradictions, and in this sense also it seems to me to hold. Working through it again, I have found the deterioration to which it pointed and of which it warned, but I have found also other kinds of movement, which are exerting their pressure in other directions. There have been, in fact, two or three marginal reforms. The reconstitution of the Press Council, which I urged in 1961, has been carried through. The Lord Chamberlain's censorship of the theatre, which I then attacked, has been abolished, though the whole censorship issue has since become much more complicated. The shopping advice centres, as a counter to advertising, and the critical broadcasting programmes, in the same area – both proposed in the first edition – are now in existence. The proposal for an extension of copyright, as a source of funds to assist contemporary writers, is again being seriously looked at. In any general view these are small gains to set against the huge losses, but they have to be noted. Then, more crucially, there has been a significant development of communications studies in education, in the schools, in further and adult education, in the polytechnics, and even in a few universities. By comparison with the situation in 1960 this is an extraordinarily encouraging development. The critical work, earlier proposed by Wells and Russell and Huxley, and notably developed by the *Scrutiny* group, has been joined by analysis of the institutions, of the kind pioneered by the New Left, and by new kinds of work, in a more closely shared orientation, on popular culture. At the same time there have been important developments in professional communications and cultural studies, in Britain and in many other countries, and there have been significant practical and theoretical advances. It is ironic that this work should have developed in the same period in which the general situation was so sharply deteriorating, but it is an instructive irony: a reminder of one of the necessary movements of history. Certainly, taken as a whole, it is a useful base for the extending work that will have to be done in the coming difficult years.

Other significant movements can be seen in this period. The sixties can now be seen as the decade of pop culture, and any analysis of that phenomenon is especially challenging. It seems to me clear that there has been an important and perhaps irreversible shift in what is seen as the cultural public. This is a further and remarkable stage of what I described in the chapter on the history of communications: an expansion of audiences which has some of the effects of a cultural revolution, but at the same time an expansion through forms of minority ownership and control which cannot wholly contradict it but which can evidently deflect and dilute it. Many more people now see the problem as the making of a democratic culture, with wide access and wide and varied participation. The older kind of defence of 'high' culture, with its associated emphasis on minority education and the social privileges needed to sustain it, has not disappeared but is now clearly residual. The real difficulty is that the worst work of the sixties, and perhaps especially the conversion of so much new popular work into commercial 'mass' routines, gives more than enough ammunition to the defenders of that old position, who warned that this would happen. There are now dangerous tendencies towards a conscious restriction of education, shared by the political parties and rationalized by reference to the economic crisis, which hold the threat of a return to the social situation in which the 'minority culture' position was plausible. Real damage will undoubtedly be done, behind a screen of references to the destructive and stupefying elements of the cultural expansion. But we have to notice, first, that the drive to restrict education is not only based on simple quantitative restriction of the expansion. It is also consciously and evidently based on a desire to reduce those parts of the educational process – notably in the arts and in social studies – on which, if in different ways, the supporters of a minority culture and of a democratic culture alike rely. Thus the campaign which is ready to use, in a negative way, the warnings and the judgements of the defenders of minority culture, will be seen – can already be seen – as consciously limiting and if possible destroying the basic elements of a humane education, in the interests of its own imperative model of a qualified bureaucracy and a graded and specialized workforce. Only the full democratic position can in the end stand against that, and this can be expected to become clearer, year by year. Meanwhile the real gains of the expansion – the new confidence of access, the new articulacy of demand, the new active qualities of resilience and opposition – are unlikely to be lost, however great the difficulties, though they are still evidently searching for new and effective social and political formations.

The commercial system, during the sixties, moved in very rapidly on every profitable movement and tendency in popular culture. It succeeded in incorporating large areas of the interests and activities of what was perceived as a new generation but was also the new cultural phase of a class. The most useful development in communications studies has been the emergence of people who belong to this phase and who are concerned and able to make necessary distinctions from inside it, and not as visitors or observers. This change was one of the major gains of the student movement of the sixties: not so much in its more publicized demonstrations as in the shift of affiliation to its generation as a whole. In recent years there has been some evident loss and reaction, but still the balance has changed. In the middle of the succeeding decade the effects of this change are still very much in play. The first five years after leaving formal education are now more than ever a critical period, for the new cultural consciousness which is active and evident while the issues are still general and theoretical is put to a severe test when people move out into a world where very different kinds of institution are waiting. The new consciousness can be put to the service of the best of the expansion. But it can also, very readily, be used by those who depend on the possession of such consciousness, in their juniors, to succeed in its profitable deflection and incorporation. I would not like to say what the likely proportions of these alternative directions will be in the coming years. The fact that one can be so often disguised as the other, and that some actual practice is genuinely mixed, makes any estimate difficult. Some new styles effectively mask old and abject kinds of surrender and hiring. Yet this at least can be said, it is hoped not cynically. The general crisis of the system, including many local and particular crises, will make many of the choices more open, even while they reduce the capacity to choose.

One of the popular diagnoses of the general crisis is that the society has become ungovernable. It is not yet true. It is primarily propaganda for still more restrictions. But it is certainly true, and in communications as clearly as anywhere, that there are new kinds of self-confidence and independence, and of loyalty to people's own real work and interests, which are fundamentally incompatible with the controlled and managed system which, under its own pressures, has to seek to control and manage yet further. The first sign of this new self-confidence and independence was the important development, in the sixties, of what was called, rather hopefully, an alternative culture. New and cheaper methods of printing led to an extraordinary development of alternative and oppositional papers and periodicals. The crisis in the commercial theatre was by-passed by many continuing experiments in community theatre, street theatre and basement theatre, and there have been similar if more scattered experiments in the more expensive media of film and television. Commercial publishing has moved into ever larger combines, but there has been an important counter-development of small independent presses and new kinds of cooperative organizations. Face to face with large organizations, groups of contributors have been organizing themselves in unprecedented ways: always under difficulties, as the history of the Free Communications Group shows, but with some significant successes: the revitalization of several of the relevant unions and associations; the formation of strong campaigns like that of the Writers' Action Group. At the same time, within the economic difficulties of the major institutions, there has been a marked increase of militancy among groups of productive workers, and an unprecedented willingness, again under major difficulties, to take direct responsibility for trying to continue an enterprise by new forms of workers' cooperatives. All these developments are so much in the spirit of my proposals for changing the institutions that I am bound to welcome them, even while I note their continuing practical and theoretical problems. The idea of an alternative culture is radical but limited. It can very easily become a marginal culture; even, at worst, a tolerated play area. It is certainly always insufficient unless it is linked with effective opposition to the dominant system, under which the majority of people are living. Again, campaigns by special interests, industrial or professional, while always necessary and in present conditions inevitable, have to be linked with serious proposals for general or specific reorganization, or they will often succeed merely in damaging one system without providing the conditions for creating a new system. In the present situation, with ever narrowing margins, this is a substantial danger, but it is of course a reason for doing more rather than doing less. One of the key developments, that of the workers' or producers' or contributors' cooperative, depends, in the high-capital areas, on active support by a reforming government, and that takes us back to one of the central areas of conflict and search. Moreover the success of any such new type of organization depends on qualities beyond the spirit of independent self-confidence which has been so evident and welcome; it depends, crucially, on kinds of skill and organization, managerial and technical as they are now normally described, which, against the grain of the system, are very difficult to acquire, to develop and to sustain. A limited militancy, within a basic acceptance of present forms of organization, is always more probable, and we must be careful not to confuse this, as we can also confuse the limited dissent of the marginal alternative culture, with the sustained and extending radicalism which is really necessary. It seems to me still to be a very open question whether clear and radical new directions, which can only be specified from working experience and from serious local planning, will be found in time, in the difficult years ahead. For there can now be no mistake about the crisis in our whole cultural organization, and in every one of our communications systems. It is easy to visualize a series of breakdowns, closures, forced sales and with them new kinds of restriction and alienation. This threat to all contributors and producers, and to the development of an extending and participating democratic culture which could perhaps once be seen as only a matter of time, has now to be taken very seriously indeed.

This is even more the case when we realize that, in the middle of a major economic crisis and preoccupied by questions of the survival of existing kinds of work, we are in fact on the threshold of a period of radical changes in communications technology. Some of these, it is true, will offer new opportunities, in simpler and cheaper equipment, and in the multiplication of channels. But if we look at the ownership of the new means and patents we soon realize that this will be no simple case of technological development under neutral social conditions. It is a complex outlook. The development of new systems of televised transmission of news and information, now under active test (the lines of light can already be seen at the top of a television screen), will bring quite new problems to the Press and to publishing. The development of cable television can bring new kinds of community broadcasting, and new opportunities for independent production, or, equally, can bring new kinds of commercial exploitation. Satellite television transmission, now a marginal support system, can become an international system beyond the control of any democratic authority, especially if it is linked with the development of domestic satellite receivers and with advertising finance from the powerful paranational companies. In certain important and popular areas like sport the first signs of such a system are already apparent, and several key conflicts are already in progress. I have discussed these developments and their problems and opportunities in my *Television: Technology and Cultural Form* (1974), and in general that book is a necessary complement to *Communications*. But I mention them here to reinforce the point that the general history and sociology of communications which I have been describing, and which has now come, evidently, to a critical point, is still profoundly active and dynamic, with new perspectives constantly opening. Moreover, though useful work is being done on the uses and problems of each of the systems, taken in isolation, it is absolutely necessary to try to see the present and probable interactions of the systems and to see these in the perspective of our general cultural development.

Looking back from 1975 I am glad that I tried to bring these issues together, in a single argument, however inadequately. The intervening years, with their different kinds of development, have shown that communications is, in modern societies, a central social, cultural and political issue. Looking forward from 1975 I believe that this will be shown to be even more true. The book written as a Special for a series on Britain in the Sixties has not only kept its relevance for Britain in the Seventies, it indicates continuing major issues, major problems and opportunities, in the world of the Seventies and Eighties. Nobody can be more conscious than I of the work that remains to be done, and the work that needs to be done better. But the book was written to initiate study, argument and action, and each of these is now even more necessary.

FURTHER READING

1 DEFINITIONS

BARNOUW, E., *Mass Communication*, New York, 1956.

BERELSON, B. and JANOWITZ, M., *Reader in Public Opinion and Communications*, Glencoe, 1953.

CHERRY, C., *On Human Communication*, London, 1957.

INNIS, H. A., *The Bias of Communication*, Toronto, 1964.

MCLUHAN, M., *Understanding Media*, New York, 1964.

WILLIAMS, R., *Television: Technology and Cultural Form*, London, 1974.

2 HISTORY

ALTICK, H. D., *The English Common Reader*, Cambridge, 1957.

BRIGGS, A., *Mass Entertainment: the origins of a modern industry*, Adelaide, 1960.

BRIGGS, A., *The Birth of Broadcasting*, London, 1961.

HERD, H., *The March of Journalism*, London, 1952.

LEAVIS, Q. D., *Fiction and the Reading Public*, London, 1932.

LOWENTHAL, L., *Literature, Popular Culture and Society*, New York, 1961.

MCLUHAN, M., *The Gutenberg Galaxy*, London, 1962.

P.E.P., *The British Film Industry*, London, 1958.

SCHILLER, H. I., *Mass Communications and American Empire*, New York, 1970.

SPRAOS, J., *Decline of the Cinema*, London, 1962.

WEBB, R. K., *The British Working Class Reader, 1796–1848*, London, 1955.

3 CONTENT

AUDIT BUREAU OF CIRCULATION, *Handbooks*, London, 1961–73.

BAKEWELL, J. and GARNHAM, N., *The New Priesthood*, London, 1970.

BLUMLER, J. G. and MCQUAIL, D., *Television in Politics*, London, 1968.

BOSTON, R. (ed.), *The Press We Deserve*, London, 1970.

CROZIER, M., *Broadcasting*, London, 1958.

DERRIEUX, E. and TEXIER, J. C., *La Presse Quotidienne Française*, Paris, 1974.

DORFMAN, A. and MATTELART, A., *How to Read Donald Duck*, New York, 1975.

FINDLATER, R., *The Unholy Trade*, London, 1952.

HALL, S. and WHANNEL, P., *The Popular Arts*, London, 1964.

HIMMELWEIT, H., OPPENHEIM, A. N. and VINCE, P., *Television and the Child*, London, 1958.

HOGGART, R., *The Uses of Literacy*, London, 1957.

HOGGART, R. (ed), *Your Sunday Paper*, London, 1967.

JACKSON, I., *The Provincial Press and the Community*, Manchester, 1971.

LAWS, F. (ed), *Made for the Million*, London, 1947.

LEAVIS, F. R. and THOMPSON, D., *Culture and Environment*, London, 1932.

MCLUHAN, M., *The Mechanical Bride*, New York, 1951.

MAYER, M., *Madison Avenue, U.S.A.*, London, 1961.

MILLUM, T., *Images of Woman*, London, 1975.

ORWELL, G., *Critical Essays*, London, 1946.

PIGASSE, J-P., *La Difficulté d'informer*, Paris, 1975.

ROSENBERG, B. and WHITE, D. M. (eds), *Mass Culture*, New York, 1958.

SMITH, A. C. H., *Paper Voices*, London, 1975.

THOMPSON, D., *Between the Lines*, London, 1939.

THOMPSON, D., *Voice of Civilization*, London, 1943.

TRENAMAN, J. and MARSDEN, D., *Television & the Political Image*, London, 1961.

TURNER, E. S., *Boys will be Boys*, Harmondsworth, 1976.

WERTHAM, F., *Seduction of the Innocent*, London, 1956.
WILLIAMS, F., *Dangerous Estate*, London, 1957.

4 CONTROVERSY and 5 PROPOSALS

BIRCH, L., *The Advertising We Deserve?*, London, 1962.
BROWN, J. A. C., *Techniques of Persuasion*, London, 1963.
ELIOT, T. S., *Notes towards the Definition of Culture*, London, 1948.
GROOMBRIDGE, B., *Television and the People*, London, 1972.
HALLORAN, J. D., *Control or Consent*, London, 1963.
HALLORAN, J. D. (ed), *The Effects of Television*, London, 1970.
HIRSCH, F. and GORDON, D., *Newspaper Money*, London, 1975.
LABOUR PARTY, *Report of the Commission on Advertising*, London, 1966.
LEAVIS, F. R., *Mass Civilisation and Minority Culture*, Cambridge, 1930.
MOONMAN, E. (ed), *The Press: a case for commitment*, London, 1969.
TUNSTALL, J. (ed), *Media Sociology*, London, 1970.
WEDELL, E. G., *Structures of Broadcasting*, Manchester, 1970.

Report of the Royal Commission on the Press, 1947–9, London.
Report of the Royal Commission on the Press, 1961–2, London.
Report of the Committee on Broadcasting, 1962, London.
Working Papers in Cultural Studies, 1–. University of Birmingham, 1971–.
The SCOB Papers, The Standing Conference on Broadcasting, London, 1976.
Future of the British Film Industry, Report of the Prime Minister's Working Party, London, 1976.